International and Local Actors in Disaster Response

International and Local Actors in Disaster Response uses the Beirut explosion in August 2020 to explore disaster prevention and response in developing states.

Disasters, whether man-made or natural, have always tested governments and their bureaucracies. Despite numerous research efforts, existing empirical literature does not provide conclusive evidence on how multiple aspects of social infrastructure can simultaneously affect disaster preparedness and recovery, and what role the international community can have. This book analyzes the role of international and local organizations in responding to the disaster in Beirut and assesses the interorganizational collaboration between the public and private sectors following the explosion. The author develops a conceptual framework of government/nonprofit relations in post-disaster management and examines the long-term disaster response and intervention of both international and local communities in a developing world context.

This book will be of interest to students, scholars, and researchers of disaster management and response, public administration, International Relations, and the nonprofit sector.

Tania N. Haddad is Assistant Professor of Public Administration in the Department of Political Studies and Public Administration at the American University of Beirut, Lebanon.

Innovations in International Affairs

Series Editor: Raffaele Marchetti, *LUISS Guido Carli, Italy*

Innovations in International Affairs aims to provide cutting-edge analyses of controversial trends in international affairs with the intent to innovate our understanding of global politics. Hosting mainstream as well as alternative stances, the series promotes both the re-assessment of traditional topics and the exploration of new aspects.

The series invites both engaged scholars and reflective practitioners, and is committed to bringing non-western voices into current debates.

Innovations in International Affairs is keen to consider new book proposals in the following key areas:

- **Innovative topics**: related to aspects that have remained marginal in scholarly and public debates
- **International crises**: related to the most urgent contemporary phenomena and how to interpret and tackle them
- **World perspectives**: related mostly to non-western points of view

Titles in this series include:

For more information about this series, please visit: http̸
.com/Innovations-in-International-Affairs/book-series/I̸

International and Local Actors in Disaster Response

Responding to the Beirut Explosion

Tania N. Haddad

Routledge
Taylor & Francis Group

LONDON AND NEW YORK

First published 2022
by Routledge
4 Park Square, Milton Park, Abingdon, Oxon OX14 4RN

and by Routledge
605 Third Avenue, New York, NY 10158

Routledge is an imprint of the Taylor & Francis Group, an informa business

© 2022 Tania N. Haddad

British Library Cataloguing-in-Publication Data
A catalogue record for this book is available from the British Library

Library of Congress Cataloging-in-Publication Data
A catalog record has been requested for this book

ISBN: 978-1-032-11990-8 (hbk)
ISBN: 978-1-032-11996-0 (pbk)
ISBN: 978-1-003-22254-5 (ebk)

DOI: 10.4324/9781003222545

Typeset in Times New Roman
by Deanta Global Publishing Services, Chennai, India

To Konstantin, Nicholas, Tatiana, and Maria

Contents

Acknowledgment

This work was fully supported by the University Research Board (Grant number: 104107- Project: 26296) at the American University of Beirut (AUB).

Introduction

Responding to disasters requires a highly dynamic network that includes coordination and collaboration between different actors – state and non-state – both at the local and international levels. While disasters are local events, the response to them is based on the role of international donors, using the best practices of international players. In this context, this local disaster directly becomes a global event (Watson, 2019). Those actors form a humanitarian community and join forces without any chain of command to respond to the disaster. From a theoretical perspective, this humanitarian aid is defined based on the United Nations General Assembly Resolution 46/182, which clearly states that humanitarian and emergency assistance will "be provided in accordance with the principles of humanity, neutrality, impartiality, and independence" (United Nations RES/46/182, 1991, p. 1). Thus, this response should de devoid of political or economic considerations and should be focused on helping individuals in emergency situations without any discrimination based on race, citizenship, or political considerations (Fink and Redaelli, 2011). Indeed, guided by humanitarianism and international politics, relief actions should be directed toward effective response for proper and faster recovery to reduce the damage and help the affected areas (Hannigan, 2012). Moreover, as per the Guidelines of the International Disaster Relief Law, Principle 10(1), this international assistance should be based on the request and consent of the affected state:

> Disaster relief or initial recovery assistance should be initiated only with the consent of the affected State and in principle, based on an appeal. The affected State should decide in a timely manner whether or not to request disaster relief or initial recovery assistance and communicate its decision promptly.

While international humanitarian assistance should be directed toward individuals in emergency situations without any other preconditions, assistance

DOI: 10.4324/9781003222545-1

is often shaped by external and global factors. In many instances, international assistance and foreign aid are grounded in political, diplomatic, and geostrategic reasons and are dominated by economic concerns. International donors, whether states and organizations, take into consideration their own benefits and agendas when responding to disasters. The influence of international factors on disaster management and on donors' contributions is reflected in the ways international order handles vulnerability, and the means by which it reproduces power relations at the international level (Watson, 2019).

From a theoretical point of view, three different strands of literature focusing on the regional and international aspects of disaster response are considerable and growing (Hanningan, 2012; Boin, Ekengren, and Rhinard, 2014; Hollis, 2015). However, there is a lack of literature that connects International Relations with disaster response (Hollis, 2018). Indeed, while literature focusing on disaster policy relates to impact of the disaster on existing diplomatic relations, most of these studies do not focus on multilevel frameworks and the relation between domestic-level issues and transnational cooperation between states (Hollis, 2018), and lack the link between these different levels of analysis.

On the domestic level, good governance plays a crucial role in managing disasters and entails

> the adoption and promotion of robust and sound policies, legislation, coordination mechanisms and regulatory frameworks, and the creation of an enabling environment that is characterized by appropriate decision-making processes to allow effective participation of stakeholders, complemented by the appropriate allocation of resources. (Jones et al., 2014; WMO, 2012)

The existing literature argues that it is governments that should coordinate all efforts in responding to disasters; indeed, most studies focus on the country's ability to counter the negative effects of a disaster. However, literature that analyzes public nonprofit relationship does not tackle the dynamics of this relation when responding to disaster.

When analyzing disaster response, a third strand focuses on the internal governance of the state. Studies have indicated that the more developed the financial system in the state and the greater its openness to trade, the more the state is building resilience to counter disasters (Toya and Skidmore, 2007). Research has also demonstrated that countries that have a high level of per capita income encounter less number of deaths during disasters (Kahn, 2005; Skidmore and Toya, 2002; Noy, 2009; Anbarci, Escaleras, and Register, 2005). In addition, the literature suggested a clear relationship between state structure and disaster response. Noy (2009) concluded that the death rate resulting from disasters is affected by the rates of literacy, size of the government, and openness to international trade: "these results suggest that the destructive potential of natural disasters can to some extent be mitigated (or exaggerated) by a country's institutions". Escaleras (2105) suggested four general categories of determinants: (1) economic factors, (2) political structure and environment, (3) social factors, and (4) historical factors. While literature on disaster management also argues that the levels of destruction caused by natural disasters are mitigated by the institutions of the country, recent studies have argued that corruption in the public sector and natural disaster are interconnected (Escaleras, Anbarci, and Register, 2007). In fact, corrupt states are affected the most in the time of natural disaster, especially in the number of death and the level of destruction, as compared to less corrupt countries (Leeson and Sobel, 2008). For example, corruption within a country's public sector would lead to increased death rates when earthquakes happen (Escaleras, Anbarci, and Register, 2007).

This research attempted to understand the dynamics behind disaster response in weak states by analyzing the three different factors stated above: (1) International Relations and the role played by international actors, (2) government–nonprofit relationship and the internal governance of the state, and (3) how the interplay between these three factors affects the response to disaster. This research at hand will address these events both in their theoretical and practical backgrounds by taking as a case study the response explosion that occurred in Beirut on August 4, 2020.

Setting the Scene: The Beirut Explosion

On August 4, 2020, two explosions rocked Beirut, the capital of Lebanon, and led to its partial destruction. A week after the explosion, the government had yet to announce a state of emergency. With the absence of government intervention in the provision of emergency relief services, international organizations, the Lebanese diaspora, local communities, organizations, and volunteers stepped in to assist and create networks to manage the disaster and help in the reconstruction phases. In line with this communitarian intervention, the international community refused to provide relief and assistance to the highly corrupt government and requested that any assistance be directly transferred to associations and affected communities.

Since the end of the civil war, the Lebanese administrative model has been based on sectarian power-sharing model that has led the state to be immersed in a regional and international power struggle for domination. Given these constant external influences, all these powers viewed the Beirut explosion as an opportunity for regional and international interference. This event increased foreign intervention and prompted the international community to call for political and economic reform, mirroring the foreign power rivalry over Lebanon that existed long before. In addition, this event changed the Lebanese political landscape and highlighted the Lebanese government's unwillingness to play a substantial role in the response and recovery phase.

A few days after the explosion, international powers started developing proposals for Lebanon, varying from economic aid to reconstruction. However, the Lebanese political system that was tainted with corruption hindered all the international efforts to help Lebanon. Indeed, this explosion highlighted the high levels of corruption in addition to the failure of a government to provide basic needs for its citizens, and the fact that it lacked the basic resources for the reconstruction and relied heavily on external support for reconstruction. This explosion also highlighted the failed Lebanese political structure, based on confessional power sharing, and its unsuitability for a modern state.

The scale of the damage went beyond the scope of the local humanitarian capability of response. Thus, international humanitarian assistance poured in. However, this aid was not presented as unconditional support. In line with this communitarian intervention, the international community refused to provide relief and assistance to the government and requested that any assistance be directly transferred to organizations and affected communities. These international donors sought the enactment of long-demanded reforms in return for financial assistance. First, the government is not considered a trustworthy partner able to manage the funds, especially as it is ranked 137th out of 198 countries in the Transparency International Corruption Index. Second, the absence of a common transparent accountable monitoring system compromises the trust of international community in handing its financial assistance. Indeed, this catastrophic event highlighted the failure of the Lebanese government in disaster management and mirrored the high levels of corruption in a system that is highly bureaucratic and highlighted the lack of trust of international organizations in the Lebanese government.

The aftermath of the disaster emphasized the intentions of regional and international stakeholders to increase the presence in the Lebanese political game. Indeed, this interference also presents another side of the problem. Lebanon has always been subject to foreign intervention, ranging from an Israeli occupation to Syrian intervention in its politics. After the explosion, both France and the United States increased their intervention and called for urgent reforms, and Lebanon was once again affected by a web of interests coming from regional and international stakeholders. Hence, it is once again important to assess the international aid for the reconstruction, which consisted of funds, medical and food supplies, to help from UN agencies, hospitals, grassroots associations, and NGOs. This assistance allowed foreign stakeholders to play a role in the reconstruction phase: both in the infrastructure as well as in the political and economic system.

This catastrophic event rose to an international event when President Macron visited Beirut and investigated the explosion area. In response, Macron called for a new political order, for "an impartial, credible and independent inquiry", and for reforms to be implemented. France also declared that the government will no longer receive direct financial support without having first regained the support and trust of the people. To receive this financial assistance, Macron noted that the Lebanese government should have a "clear and transparent governance" to ensure international aid goes directly to the people affected by the explosion.

Macron's program listed four sectors in need of immediate attention: humanitarian aid and a response to the COVID-19 pandemic; physical reconstruction from the blast; political and economic reforms; and early parliamentary elections. The French government also called for the immediate resumption of talks with the IMF for loans. In parallel, the White House called for transparency, reform, and accountability. On the 9th of August, with the United Nations, France co-organized an international conference for international aid for Lebanon. This event was attended by world leaders and government officials, whereby 36 countries pledged $300 million for emergency support.

Concurrently, international organizations were faced with three different options: (1) relying on a corrupt government to channel disbursement, (2) maintaining control over the funding decisions by risking criticism of foreign influence, or (3) not assisting altogether. As such, they presented a new model labeled: "Reform, Recovery, and Reconstruction Framework", to ensure proper distribution of funds, and to pool all donations into a system with proper structure to empower civil society by channeling funds directly toward nongovernmental organizations. This framework would allow Lebanese organizations to be part of the steering committee that governs the funds and to have a crucial role in monitoring the implementation.

More than a year and a half after the explosion, despite international and local efforts to help rehouse the victims of the explosion, the area has not recovered, and some Lebanese citizens and residents remain homeless. Indeed, the relief process was not successful: in the total absence of the state, associations in Lebanon were alone to respond to the disaster, and the lack of cooperation, coordination and planning, and funding led to the failure in reconstructing the city, and in responding to the disaster. This bottom-up approach to the management of the issue was faced with failure (Fawaz and Harb, 2020).

The above patterns can be viewed from political lenses rather than humanitarian needs only: foreign policies and domestic policies, realpolitik, and security affect the allocation of funds and the response to the disaster (Walker et al., 2008).

Main Aim

This study proposes to introduce a new perspective in looking at disaster management and response from an international perspective. By taking the Beirut explosion as a case study, it assesses the crucial role of international communities, civil society, nonprofit associations, and their relationship with the state in responding to the disaster. This research fills the gap in the literature about the role of international and local communities in disaster prevention and response in light of a weak state and the link between International Relations and disaster response. Despite numerous research efforts, the empirical literature does not provide conclusive evidence on how multiple aspects of the social infrastructure can simultaneously affect disaster response and recovery, and what role can international community play, which is the primary aim of this study.

This study will examine the role of international and local actors in changing and shaping the response to disaster in the light of a developing state. Theoretically, this study extends an existing multidimensional model of collaboration into the context of emergency management, and it addresses three major questions:

A. What role do international community, civil society, and local communities play in response to disasters?
   - What strategies did they use?
   - What was the economic and social impact of these community-based approaches?
   - What lessons did we learn?
B. What were the barriers and enablers of interorganizational collaboration between the international community and organization and public sectors in disaster response in the Beirut explosion?
C. What was the long-term impact of this intervention?

The main argument presented is that aid in disaster response is a transboundary phenomenon that would either promote cooperation or intensify conflict among international players. Building on the conceptual frameworks developed by Marchetti et al. (2009), Salamon and Anheier (1998), Young (1999, 2000), Najam (2000), and Haddad (2017) on government–nonprofit relationship, this research suggests the development of new public–private interorganizational partnership post-disaster response in Lebanon. It will further explore the different negative and positive aspects of such interorganizational collaboration by aligning the findings with the five dimensions of collaboration described by Thomson, Perry, and Miller (2009) and Curnin and O'Hara (2019).

Division of the Remainder of the Book

To fill the gap in the literature on disaster management in International Relations, Chapter 1 examines the role of international actors (state and nonstate) in responding to disasters, and explores their roles, responsibilities, their governance struggles, and their effect, in addition to the role of politics in this area, specifically in the context of the developing world. It will review the role of the international community in disaster response whether states, diaspora, intergovernmental organization, or international nongovernmental agencies.

This chapter will also address disaster response as functional cooperation used by international players, mainly states, to advance their personal internal interests. In addition, this chapter will explore in depth governance struggles in the context of the developing world, where different international players and stakeholders emerge to fill the gap left by a weak government. Chapter 1 argues that although international humanitarian assistance should be directed toward helping individuals in emergency situations without any discrimination based on race, citizenship, or political considerations, the reality is different. It will review how international assistance and foreign aid are mainly based on strategic, political, diplomatic, and geostrategic reasons. International donors from states and organizations take into considerations their own benefits and agendas when responding to disasters. It argues that in developing countries, the role of these international players is crucial for the relief efforts. Moreover, this chapter will review the ways some international aid emphasizes the failure of the affected governments in managing disasters and how the reliance of these international donors would lead to limited commitment on the part of the affected state and weak governance of local institutions.

Chapter 2 reviews the role of local players in disaster management. There is a vast literature on disaster management and prevention in democratic countries. However, few have discussed the effects of corruption on natural and man-made disasters. As such, this chapter will review three strands of literature. First, it will analyze the relationship between corruption and disaster prevention. Second, it will discuss the role of social capital in disaster management. Third, it will review the literature on the nonprofit sector and disaster response in the light of a failed state.

Chapter 3 will set the scene leading to the explosion and will review the literature on public administration, disaster response corruption, and the historical role of organizations in responding to disaster in Lebanon. This chapter will first argue that the apocalyptic event highlighted the culture of negligence, corruption, and blame shift that characterize the Lebanese bureaucracy, which also highly depends on volunteers and the nonprofit sector to fill the gap. It will argue that while many international initiatives were presented to help the government on the issue of transparency, management techniques, and focus on information technology in service delivery, most of these initiatives were constrained by the political system in the state (Bhuiyan et al., 2020). In addition, these initiatives were constrained by the dysfunctional political system (Antoun, 2008; Makdisi, Kiwan, and Marktanner, 2010; Salamey, 2014; Haase, 2018), especially as it does not allow individual citizens to participate in the decision-making process and allows political parties to establish clientelist relationships that supersede people's demands (Makdisi et al., 2010; Safa, 2010; Haase, 2018). This chapter will also review the disaster management response and the lack of response to the different disasters in Lebanon. The government failed to respond to disasters and withdrew from the recovery phase, leaving space for different actors to support the society.

Chapter 4 reviews the international response to the Beirut explosion: it further analyzes the role played by each of the different international players and their impact on Lebanese citizens. It will review the ways international order handled the vulnerability of the state and how responding to the event reproduced power sharing at the international level. Moreover, this chapter will argue that international response to the explosion was indeed shaped by global factors, and humanitarian assistance varied between different players: the assistance, and sometimes lack of assistance, by the international players highlighted the weaknesses of the state and undermined its credibility. To understand the role of international players in disaster response, and the relationship with the state, qualitative data were collected through a series of semi-structured interviews (Krueger and Casey, 2015) with IR theorists in addition to associations and initiatives that responded to the post-explosion.

Chapter 5 reviews the role of local players in responding to the Beirut explosion. Lebanon has always relied on its civil society in critical times due to the absence of the state in responding to disasters. This active civil society is the result of the absence of the state in different critical circumstances. After the Beirut Port explosion, Lebanese volunteers and civil society were the first to intervene long before international aids started coming to Lebanon (Chehayeb and Sewell, 2020). Local NGOs and initiatives with the help of social media launched several campaigns to help people whose houses were damaged find shelters (Ghantous, 2021). Chapter 5 will further assess the interorganizational relationship that appeared between the different players at the local level.

References

Anbarci, N., Escaleras, M., & Register, C. A. (2005). Earthquake fatalities: The interaction of nature and political economy. *Journal of Public Economics, 89*(9–10), 1907–1933.

Antoun, R. (2008). *Towards a national anti-corruption strategy.* Beirut: The Lebanese Transparency Association.

Bhuiyan, S., & Farazmand, A. (2020). Society and public policy in the Middle East and North Africa. *International Journal of Public Administration, 43*(5), 373–377.

Boin, A., Rhinard, M., & Ekengren, M. (2014). Managing transboundary crises: The emergence of European Union capacity. *Journal of Contingencies and Crisis Management, 22*(3), 131–142.

Chehayeb, K., & Sewell, A. (2020). Local groups step up to Lead Beirut blast response. *The New Humanitarian.* Last modified August 18, 2020. https://www.thenewhumanitarian.org/news-feature/2020/08/18/Lebanon-Beirut-explosion-local-aid-response.

Curnin, S., & O'Hara, D. (2019). Nonprofit and public sector interorganizational collaboration in disaster recovery: Lessons from the field. *Nonprofit Management and Leadership, 30*(2), 277–297.

Escaleras, M., Anbarci, N., & Register, C. A. (2007). Public sector corruption and major earthquakes: A potentially deadly interaction. *Public Choice, 132*(1), 209–230.

Fawaz, M., & Harb, M. (2020). Is Lebanon becoming another "Republic of the NGOs"? *BeirutUrbanLab.* Last modified October 13, 2020. https://beiruturbanlab.com/Details/697.

Fink, G., & Redaelli, S. (2011). Determinants of international emergency aid—Humanitarian need only? *World Development, 39*(5), 741–757.

Haase, T. W. (2018). A challenging state of affairs: Public administration in the republic of Lebanon. *International Journal of Public Administration, 41*(10), 792–806.

Haddad, T. (2017). Analyzing state–civil society associations relationship: The case of Lebanon. *Voluntas: International Journal of Voluntary and Nonprofit Organizations, 28*(4), 1742–1761.

Hannigan, J. (2012). *Disasters without borders.* Cambridge: Polity, 97–110.

Hollis, S. (2015). *The role of regional organizations in disaster risk management.* Basingstoke: Palgrave Macmillan.

Hollis, S. (2018). Bridging international relations and disaster studies: The case of disaster-conflict scholarship. *Disasters, 42*(1), 19–40. https://doi.org/10.1111/disa.12231.

Jones, S., Oven, K. J., Manyena, B., & Aryal, K. (2014). Governance struggles and policy processes in disaster risk reduction: A case study from Nepal. *Geoforum, 57,* 78–90.

Kahn, M. E. (2005). The death toll from natural disasters: The role of income, geography, and institutions. *Review of Economics and Statistics, 87*(2), 271–284.

Krueger, R. A., and Casey, M. A. (2015). *Focus groups: A practical guide for applied research.* Thousand Oaks, CA: Sage Publications.

Leeson, P. T., & Sobel, R. S. (2008). Weathering corruption. *Journal of Law and Economics, 51*(4), 667–681.

Makdisi, S., Kiwan, F., & Marktanner, M. (2010). 'Lebanon: The constrained democracy and its national impact', In I. Elbadawi & S. Makdisi (Eds.), *Democracy in the Arab world: Explaining the deficit* (pp. 115–141). New York: Routledge.

Marchetti, R., & Tocci, N. (2009). Conflict society: Understanding the role of civil society in conflict. *Global Change, Peace and Security, 21*(2), 201–217.

Najam, A. (2000). The four Cs of government third sector-government relations. *Nonprofit Management and Leadership, 10*(4), 375–396.

Noy, I. (2009). The macroeconomic consequences of natural disasters. *Journal of Development Economics, 88*(2), 221–231.

Safa, O. (2010). Lebanon. In J. Dizzard, C. Walker & S. Cook (Eds.), *Countries at the crossroads: An analysis of democratic governance* (pp. 341–360). New York: Freedom House.

Salamey, I. (2014). *The government and politics of Lebanon.* New York: Routledge.

Salamon, L. M., & Anheier, H. K. (1998). Social origins of civil society: Explaining the nonprofit sector cross-nationally. *Voluntas: International Journal of Voluntary and Nonprofit Organizations, 9*(3), 213–248.

Skidmore, M., & Toya, H. (2002). Do natural disasters promote long-run growth? *Economic Inquiry, 40*(4), 664–687.

Thomson, A. M., Perry, J. L., & Miller, T. K. (2009). Conceptualizing and measuring collaboration. *Journal of Public Administration Research and Theory, 19*(1), 23–56.

Toya, H., & Skidmore, M. (2007). Economic development and the impacts of natural disasters. *Economics Letter, 94*(1), 20–25.

United Nations RES/46/182. (1991). Strengthening of the coordination of humanitarian emergency assistance of the United Nations. p. 1.

Walker, P., & Maxwell, D. (2008). *Shaping the humanitarian world.* London: Routledge.

Watson, S. D. (2019). *International order and the politics of disaster.* New York, New York, U.S.A.: Routledge.

WMO. (2012). *Disaster risk reduction (DRR) program.* World Meteorological Organization (WMO). http://www.wmo.int/pages/prog/drr/DRRFramework_en .htm (accessed 04.07.14).

Young, D. R. (1999). Complementary, supplementary, or adversarial? A theoretical and historical examination of nonprofit-government relations in the United States. In Boris, E.T. & Steuerle, C.E. (Eds.), *Nonprofits and government:*

Collaboration and conflict (pp. 31–67). Washington, D.C.: The Urban Institue Press.

Young, D. R. (2000). Alternative models of government-nonprofit sector relations: Theoretical and international perspectives. *Nonprofit and Voluntary Sector Quarterly, 29*(1), 149–172.

1 International Relations, Diplomacy, and International Players in Disaster Response

Introduction

The available literature on International Relations (IR) has rarely touched on the field of disaster management. Some scholars in the field have stated that International Relations considers assisting in responding to any disaster as independent from politics (Hannigan, 2012; Watson, 2019). When reviewing the available literature on International Law, it was apparent that the field suffers from a dearth of research on disaster response, as this topic has been less addressed than other issues (Nishimoto, 2014). Moreover, when the literature does address disaster response, it does not tackle the role played by different stakeholders in disaster response, and the data are not inclusive on whether disasters can increase intra- or interstate conflict or whether a disaster can lead to rapprochement between two sides of a conflict.

Building bridges between IR and disaster can be studied through three theoretical frames: realism, neorealism, and liberalism. Realism posits that the state is the highest authority, that the international system is composed of states and is ruled by anarchy (Weber, 2010). Conflicts can occur when a population and individuals fear for their lives from another state (Hollis, 2018). Neorealism is based on the idea that in an anarchy, states always seek power when their survival is threatened. Therefore, when states lack resources when disasters strike, this scarcity can push states to conflicts (Barnett, 2007). Liberalism reflects an opposite aspect of International Relations theory. Liberalism states that uncertainties can create a sort of rapprochement and generate a ground for discussion and cooperation which solve conflicts instead of creating new ones (Hollis, 2015).

To fill the gap in the literature on disaster management in International Relations, this chapter will examine the role of international actors (state and nonstate) in responding to disasters, and will explore their roles, responsibilities, their governance struggles, and their effects in addition to

DOI: 10.4324/9781003222545-2

the role of politics in this area, specifically in the context of the developing world. This chapter will also address disaster response as functional cooperation used by international players, mainly states, to advance their personal internal interests. In addition, this chapter will explore in depth the governance struggles in the context of the developing world, where different international players and stakeholders emerge to fill the gap in response left by a weak government. As such, this chapter raises the following questions: what is the role of international players (being state and nonstate actors) in disaster relief in a developing context? To what extent do the personal agendas of donors affect disaster response? The main argument of this chapter is that aid in disaster response is a transboundary phenomenon that would either promote cooperation or intensify conflict among international players, and as such, international assistance and foreign aid are conditioned by strategic, political, diplomatic, and geostrategic reasons and are dominated by economic concerns. To do so, this chapter is divided into five sections: the first section "What Is International Humanitarian Assistance", defines international humanitarian assistance, the second section "Intergovernmental and Regional Organizations", reviews the role of international and regional interstate organizations, the third section "International Nongovernmental Organizations (INGOs)", discusses the role of International NGOs (INGOs), the fourth section "Role of Diaspora", discusses the political and social role of diaspora, and the fifth section "Role Diplomacy and Donor States in Disaster Response", discusses diplomacy and disaster response while focusing on state donors.

What Is International Humanitarian Assistance

Responding to disasters requires a highly dynamic network that includes coordination and collaboration between different actors being state and nonstate, both at the local and international levels. While disasters are local events, the response to them is based on the role of international donors and through the best practices of INGOs and multinational corporations (Watson, 2019). In this context, this local disaster directly becomes a global event (Watson, 2019). Those actors that form a humanitarian community join forces without any chain of command to respond to the disaster. As argued in the introduction of this book, from a theoretical perspective, the definition of this type of humanitarian aid is based on the United Nations General Assembly Resolution 46/182, which clearly states that humanitarian and emergency assistance should be based on the principles of humanity, neutrality, impartiality, and independence (United Nations RES/46/182, 1991, p. 1). Indeed, guided by humanitarianism, relief actions should be directed toward effective response for proper and faster recovery to reduce the damage and help the damaged areas (Hannigan, 2012).

These humanitarian organizations take on various structures: they may vary from international governmental organizations to supranational aid agencies (such as UN agencies) (Wei et al., 2019). Each of these organizations has different missions, interests, and expertise (Balcik et al., 2010; Wei et al., 2019) and its roles differ from the ones performed by local players: for example, while grassroots organizations might focus on assisting on one specific group (Beamon and Balcik, 2008; Kovács and Spens, 2008), international players would focus on the whole affected area.

The International Federation of Red Cross and Red Crescent Societies (IFRC) argues that international agencies should supplement the efforts of national actors in disaster management and should interfere once local efforts are exhausted or when the state is unwilling to act (Walker et al., 2008). In 2007, and in response to many instances where international response was delayed by national policies and states' inability to deal with the demands of international relief teams, the IFRC developed international guidelines, known as the International Disaster Response Law (IDRL). The aim of the IDRL was to develop best practices in disaster relief; assist states in strengthening their disaster response and management policies, and highlight the importance of implementing relief programs responsibly to ensure proper response and better accountability for donors. These goals were consistent with IFRC's main goals, which include ensuring that "people anticipate, respond to, and quickly recover from crisis" (IFRC, 2021).

Moreover, as per the IDRL Guidelines, Principle 10(1) this international assistance should be based on the request and consent of the affected state:

> Disaster relief or initial recovery assistance should be initiated only with the consent of the affected State and in principle, on the basis of an appeal. The affected State should decide in a timely manner whether or not to request disaster relief or initial recovery assistance and communicate its decision promptly. In order to make this decision, the affected State should promptly assess needs. Consideration should be given to undertaking joint needs assessments with the United Nations and other assisting humanitarian organizations.

The nature of humanitarian organizations and the method with which they implement their relief services affect donation channels and amounts. Some donor countries decide to provide donations in kind or rely on other organizations to implement relief projects. However, irrespective of the process or nature of the service, these humanitarian actors are restricted by four principles when responding to disasters. These include humanity, impartiality, neutrality, and independence (Cook et al., 2018). Given these principles, the emergency relief responses of humanitarian organizations should be based on human rights and on the principle of "do no harm" and on impartiality, irrespective of economic or political purposes.

Despite the presence of these principles, a lot of criticism has been directed toward international aid policies (Darcy and Hofmann, 2003; IFRC, 2003; Olsen et al., 2003; Walker et al., 2005; Fink and Redaelli, 2011). Indeed, when examining literature on donations from the international community, it is revealed that assistance is mostly based on strategic and political reasons and is usually dominated by economic concerns (Olsen et al., 2003; Barthelemy and Tichit, 2004; Drury et al., 2005; Wei et al., 2014). Therefore, while developing and developed countries receive international assistance when affected by disasters, response from international community is never the same: donors, countries, and organizations have their own agendas and policies when it comes to disaster response (Wei, 2019). Affected countries differ in socioeconomic status in addition to regional and global influence (Wei, 2019), and as such, the global relief responses also differ in their donations, initiatives, and responses to these disasters. This means that the decision to donate and the amount of the donation would be determined based on the extent to which these would advance the donors' agendas in the affected country. In this case, donations would not be need-based, falling out of line with their guiding principles.

Another point that needs to be raised is the effect of this response on the internal politics of the affected state. While international assistance does provide financial help to domestic governments, this assistance affects the domestic politics of the latter (Attina, 2012), especially in light of the political and international factors affecting aid allocation and the conditions placed for governments to be able to receive aid. This type of assistance highlights the weaknesses of the government and undermines its credibility as a result (Olson and Gawronski, 2010: 218). In fact, international aid can highlight the failure of the government in disaster preparedness and response and could lead the public to assess the competence of their governments in disaster response as compared to international donors (Attina, 2012). In poor and developing countries, international actors play a crucial role in disaster management, especially where disaster expertise is lacking (Rajan, 2002). In the absence of financial and nonfinancial resources, assistance from countries and international players becomes crucial for disaster survivors in building resilience (Wei et al., 2019). However, this supply-driven reliance on international donor could lead to weak governance within local institutions, limited commitment from the state, and disordered decision-making at the local level (Godfrey et al., 2002). This international aid can negatively affect states' institutions since it allows them to become dependent on international donations in the long run and would diminish the state's commitment to respond to the disaster. Moreover, international humanitarian organizations have their own norms and conditional procedures for the distribution of aid which would limit the recipient governments' ability to gain political credit (Attina, 2012).

This section has argued that although international aid should only be based on humanitarian response, many other factors are taken into consideration when deciding on the response approach. In this regard, the next section will review the role of intergovernmental and regional organizations in disaster response.

Intergovernmental and Regional Organizations

Intergovernmental organizations that have sovereign states as members are known as multilateral organizations. They are formed under a charter of rules and responsibilities and play a crucial role in disaster response. These can be regionally based, such as the European Union (EU), or can be organized around one common issue such as the North Atlantic Treaty Organization (NATO), or can be globally based, such as the United Nations. These intergovernmental organizations enjoy a legal status under international law (Coppola, 2015). Historically, the first international organization that addressed disaster management was the International Relief Union (IRU), founded in 1921 (Coppola, 2015). Since then, many new organizations have taken the role of assistance, mainly the United Nations and the International Monetary Fund, which will be discussed below.

United Nations' Role in Disaster Management and Response

The United Nations is viewed as the organization that is most prepared to be involved in every aspect of disaster management cycle. This organization is viewed as having strong ties with most of the countries and as having a strong presence in developing countries where most disasters strike hard. In these areas, the UN works on the development of disaster risk reductions (DRRs) to help states build resilience. The UN is also the main player for technical and financial relief aid such as shelter and medical assistance when disaster strikes. The main office responsible for disaster response is the UN Office of the Coordination of Humanitarian Affairs (OCHA). The role of this office is divided into three categories (Coppola, 2015): (1) organizing all international relief efforts, (2) working on policy proposals and development at the international level, and (3) advocating for proper relief policies directed toward peace building. Historically, this type of organization has played a crucial response in the different levels of disaster management. International financial institutions are also crucial players in disaster management.

International Financial Institutions

These institutions are made up of states on a global level that cooperate to provide financial assistance to governments. Their main aim is to provide loans for developmental projects in national governments and to ensure financial stability and political balance. The main role that these organizations play is to offer assistance in post-disaster reconstruction in developing countries with access to low capital resources, without which these latter would be incapable of recovering. The major institutions are the World Bank and its subsidiary and the International Monetary Fund (IMF).

The World Bank

This institution is speared in 188 states and comprises different institutions and is the largest supporter in development assistance. It is the main provider of post-disaster, humanitarian emergency financial reconstructions, and loans for essential programs. France was the first country to receive postwar reconstruction assistance from the World Bank in 1947 with a loan of around 250 million dollars. Today, developing countries endure the most post-disaster as they are the least prepared and tend to lack mitigation policy.

International Monetary Fund (IMF)

The main goal of the IMF is to "promote international monetary cooperation, exchange stability and orderly exchange arrangements; to foster economic growth and high levels of employment; and to provide temporary financial assistance to countries to help ease balance of payments adjustment" (https://www.imf.org). Thus far, the IMF has assisted more than 180 countries that were affected by disasters and emergencies by providing them with financial aid. The IMF provides support through a comprehensive strategy by promoting the establishment of a stable government that can implement a sound and clear economic plan based on proper reconstruction process. The IMF also provides technical assistance for governments post-disaster to help them implement macroeconomic policies such as monetary and fiscal policies.

Regional Organizations

These organizations usually focus on or address disaster management and provide financial and technical resources. One of the most significant players and active stakeholders in international humanitarian assistance has been the European Union. The EU has also structured itself to be an active stakeholder in international disaster management. In this regard, its work is not limited to Europe and has a global presence. The EU initiated humanitarian assistance from 1992 and has grown to provide around 50% of worldwide humanitarian aid. It has also responded to disasters through one or more of its various departments in more than 140 countries (Coppola, 2015).

The League of Arab States (LAS) and Regional Centre for Disaster Risk Reduction (RCDRR)

The first Arab strategy for DRR was adopted in 2010. This strategy was aligned with the global priorities set by Hyogo Framework for Action (HFA) and the Millennium Development Goals. The main role of this strategy was to complement the existing plans at the national levels and had two main aims: (1) to set up a vision and strategic plan for disaster risk reduction in the region, and (2) to strengthen the coordination mechanism for the implementation of this strategy and the establishment of programs of actions. Since the main challenge facing the region is the lack of funding, the LAS has stressed upon its members to invest 1% of their national development funding to risk reduction policies.

International Nongovernmental Organizations

INGOs are major players in the international humanitarian system: they can be transnational having a budget of major corporations or even states and can represent ranges of interests and approaches. For different reasons, whether geographical or political, donor states and organizations might be reluctant to deliver donations in cash or in kind to affected areas and countries (Wei et al., 2019). The role of humanitarian organizations as a major player linking donors to recipients is most visible in these circumstances (Wei et al., 2019). Moore et al. (2003) argued that humanitarian organizations' decisions to coordinate with International NGOs is based on the expertise of INGOs as well as the role they play in the humanitarian aid network. International nongovernmental organizations are usually more focused on providing relief in large-scale disasters, or one type of relief or even aiding for specific groups of target communities (Kovács and Spens, 2008). To name a few, the International Federation of Red Cross and Crescent Societies are focused on offering leadership to the humanitarian community in emergency shelters as well as consolidating best practices in addition to leading coordinated responses (Wei, 2019). The Norwegian and Finnish Red Cross organizations offer field hospitals, and the Canadian and Danish Red Cross groups provide logistical support (Wei, 2019). It was in the 1990s that the role of INGOs started to increase at the international level and play a crucial role in disaster preparedness and response and are the backbone of the international humanitarian system (Walker et al., 2008). NGOs and UN agencies started organizing in a more professional manner, establishing global standards for their activities. Indeed, most of the funds of the humanitarian agencies of the United Nations are channeled via INGOs.

Estimating the annual budget of INGOs is nearly impossible as these organizations do not consolidate their financials in a transparent manner that is accessible to the public. Moreover, they have different sections, branches, and members, which makes it difficult to account for their budgetary importance. Sometimes these organizations report different figures for development projects and humanitarian ones. Walker et al. (2008) compared the annual reports of major NGOs vis-à-vis the UN and the Red Cross movements and argued that the largest INGOs working on the ground in financial sizes are the World Vision, CARE, Save the Children, Oxfam, and MSF.

Walker et al. (2008) identified five different trends in the work of these organizations:

1. Adapting to structures: Many INGOs were national organizations that moved to a transnational status. For example, to do so, World Vision transformed its local branches in the south to autonomous organizations under a federated structure of World Vision International. Thus, most of the INGOs are under a form of federation or international alliance.
2. Central to humanitarian work: Due to the growth of these organizations, they have become crucial players in humanitarian intervention, while previously they were viewed as side players in the system. These organizations are now represented through different umbrellas such as InterAction, the International Council for Voluntary Agencies (ICVA), and the Steering Committee for Humanitarian Response (SCHR) on the Inter-Agency Standing Committee. These INGOS can have direct access to UN Security Council meetings and can also lobby different governments.
3. Cooptation: These organizations are co-opted by global humanitarian agendas as well as by narrower agendas that support western as well as northern foreign policies.
4. Shift toward professionalism: The major role of NGOs as a voluntary charitable sector has shifted toward a professional status. This transformation is mainly due to their increasing role in humanitarian work and their crucial role in developing international standards. These

changes lead to a question about the shift in mission and about financial accountability.

5. Funding issues: Because of the increasing corporate structure being imposed on these NGOs, these latter have lost the basis of their importance: being able to tailor response and program to the context of the crisis. Due to funding opportunities and to secure funds from governments, these associations have changed their tailor-made programs to more standardized programs, leading to many failures in implementation.

As presented above, these international nongovernmental organizations are major players in disaster response. For different reasons, donor states opt to assist through these organizations as opposed to directly assisting the affected state. These different organizations play a role in leading the response as well as in providing logistical support and adapt to the environment and the type of disasters. Through their response, these organizations can represent the interest and agendas of donor organizations and states.

Role of Diaspora

Another important player at the international level is the diaspora. To understand the role of diaspora, it is important to provide a general definition of the term. While sociologists, anthropologists, and political scientists differ in their definition of the term (Bostrom et al., 2016), the term diaspora can most commonly be defined as a connotation of a strong bond with the homeland based on shared memory and experience and a collective memory of the homeland. Van Hear et al. (2004:3) define diaspora "as populations of migrant origin who are scattered among two or more destinations, between which there develop multifarious links involving flows and exchanges of people and resources: between the homeland and destination countries, and among destination countries". The diaspora plays a crucial role in disaster response, whether through direct financial support or through the mobilization of strategic political actions (Naik et al., 2007). The level of involvement differs based on the socioeconomic status of the diaspora itself and the level of attachment to their homeland (Naik et al., 2007).

While, historically, the primary role of the diaspora involved voluntary work, as well as direct monetary or in-kind support to family and friends and sometimes NGOs, this role has recently developed to make this type of actor a crucial player in disaster response and coordination at the international level. With the development in technology, financial transactions, and communications, the international humanitarian system that includes many players, such as agencies within the United Nations, the International

Red Cross and Red Crescent and western NGOs, started understanding the importance of the role of diaspora in responding to disasters in their home countries (Bostrom et al., 2016). As such, given the increased importance of the diaspora in disaster response, this section will review the literature on the role of diaspora to investigate the important role of this new player in disaster response.

Diaspora Networks

Diaspora networks are a crucial player in disaster responses (Bostrom et al., 2016). When responding to disaster, the diaspora organizes itself into networks that can be informal, such as a set of relationships that connects the members to family and friends in the mother country. The diaspora network can also be formal and can be based on agreements between individuals and organizations that collaborate for a main purpose (Bostrom et al., 2016). While the major role of the diaspora during a disaster is to send monetary donations, this community also plays a major advocacy role on behalf of the affected population at the global and transnational levels (Bell, 2010). For example, many diasporas organize in Hometown Associations (HTAs), where groups of people who originate from the same town or village share a common interest in supporting their community back home and establishing self-organizations (Bell, 2010). Moreover, the diaspora is active in faith-based organizations as these organizations become a main point for meetings to mobilize resources when disaster strikes (Hammond et al., 2011). Both faith-based organizations and HTAs exist before the disaster, and thus mobilization of resources around them becomes easy when disaster strikes. While HTAs and communities in the faith-based organizations can act directly when disaster strikes, these efforts and capabilities are usually restrained by the absence of capabilities and information regarding the affected areas. Thus, this limitation in information could sometimes lead to duplication of efforts on the ground (Hammond et al., 2011).

Monetary Support or Remittances

Most of the literature on the role of the diaspora in development focused on the role of donation support, For example, by 2010, the donation to developing countries reached around US$325 billion every year, and this number represented twice the donated amount by foreign countries through the overseas development assistance (ODA) (Kleist and Vammen, 2012). Thus, these remittances come as a crucial support for the affected community and usually increase when the homeland faces economic crises and financial as well as political instability. These remittances help sustain the lives of the affected community as well as "stimulate the operation of markets affected by the shock at local level" (Naik et al., 2007:46). These remittances are crucial for emergency and reconstruction processes (Naik et al., 2007), and they have both social and cultural values in addition to their economic values. In addition to these remittances, the diaspora usually collects funds and basic products for relief efforts and are a driving force in advocating for official assistance to their homeland through their mobilization and communication strategies.

However, while this support can be quickly mobilized, it is usually a short-term direct response, and the donations might be misplaced due to the absence of an effective channel for response in the affected community and inside the affected state (Naik et al., 2007). Moreover, the efficiency and effectiveness of the assistance is usually questioned since most diaspora are not experts in disaster response or do not have an objective view of the needs of the affected community and most of the resources are usually directed to one activity, which signifies a lack of proper planning for disaster recovery (Naik et al., 2007). It is also argued that remittances, on some occasions, affect political accountability as they allow certain groups to rule despite their failure to properly govern their areas of power (Lindley, 2006).

Volunteerism and Diaspora

Remittances are one type of support from the diaspora. Another type of engagement is usually seen through volunteering. The diaspora assists by sharing information, skills, and connections through social networks (Bostrom et al., 2016). During disasters, volunteers serve as first responders and return to the affected areas to share their expertise and skills (King and Grullon, 2013) even before the mobilization of traditional humanitarian organizations. This diaspora plays a crucial role as intermediaries between humanitarian actors and the affected community (Meier, 2013; Sahloul, 2014; Sida, 2014; Bostrom et al., 2016). For instance, international organizations tend to recruit relief staff from diaspora communities to better respond to humanitarian crises, especially in conflict countries such as Iraq and Syria (Steets et al., 2012); and sometimes, diaspora also assist local NGOs in the coordination of donations and the development of best practices (Sahloul, 2014).

Technology and communication also play a crucial role in the involvement of the diaspora in disaster relief. Indeed, virtual organization allowed for financial and human mobilization across international borders (Meier, 2011; Meier, 2013; King and Grullon, 2013) and enabled the diaspora to further play the role of intermediary between the affected population and humanitarian organizations.

In conclusion, while diasporas play a crucial role in disaster response, they have both financial and sociopolitical effects. However, to better help with the affected populations, international actors, relief agencies, and donors should coordinate more with these diasporas through reaching out to either individuals, HTAs, or churches (Fagen, 2006, p. 15).

Role Diplomacy and Donor States in Disaster Response

Literature on international assistance provided by states argues that international assistance is multifaced and considers the characteristics of affected countries (Wei and Marinova, 2016). This international assistance is based on many factors, such as the (1) socioeconomic development of the state concerned, the (2) political and diplomatic effect of the assistance, and (3) the economic benefit for the donor state, in addition to the geostrategies of the different parties (Wei et al., 2019).

Reviewing the motives behind the donations provided by donor governments in international crises will allow us to understand why some crises and disasters are better funded than others and why some donations are often directed toward international and local NGOs as opposed to governments. In international law, for foreign states to send military and civilian assistance post-disaster, they should abide by a legal basis for deployment. This legal basis is based on three sources (Telec, 2014): (1) the right of sovereignty and territorial integrity, (2) the customary law of noninterference in domestic affairs of another entity, and (3) the principle of nonuse of force.

Moreover, to intervene, the consent of the affected state should be provided based on the idea of respect of sovereignty and compliance with international law, as mentioned on several occasions by the General Assembly UN Document in 1991:

> The sovereignty, territorial integrity and national unity of States must be fully respected in accordance with the Charter of the United Nations. In this context, humanitarian assistance should be provided with the consent of the affected country and in principle on the basis of an appeal by the affected country. (https://undocs.org/A/RES/46/182)

To assist the affected state, the latter should secure immunity for deployed personnel. In addition, the recipient state should be able to balance between its sovereign interests, and at the same time protect the deployed personnel from liability and regulatory barriers (Telec, 2014).

Walker et al. (2008) argue that most of the international humanitarian assistance comes from western governments: with the United States around 33% of global government funding (in 2005); followed by the EU with

15%, then Japan, France, and the United Kingdom with an average of 6% each. This assistance is highly clustered in terms of sources and services. The biggest sector for humanitarian expenditure remains the global food aid with around 40% of global humanitarian expenditures in 2005, while other sectors such as health and protection received around 10% of the global fund (Walker et al., 2008). However, when it comes to the type and amount of assistance, things change. European countries' decisions to help are based on cosmopolitan humanitarianism (Wei et al., 2019), which is based on the principle of military intervention with the aim of assisting vulnerable populations.

The above patterns can be viewed from an International Relations lens rather than from humanitarian needs only: foreign policies and domestic policies, realpolitik and security affect the allocation of funds (Walker et al., 2008). Indeed, the type of assistance from foreign actors is highly based on political and strategic considerations (Wei et al., 2019; Annen and Strickland, 2017; Zagefka and James, 2015). Thus, when studying disaster response, it is important to address the political agendas and motivations of donor states to be able to identify the conditions placed on donations, albeit sometimes unofficial, which are contrary to the principle of humanitarianism in this context.

When responding to disasters, donor states usually focus on maximizing their power in International Relations (Morgenthau, 1978; Zhang, 2006; Wei et al., 2014). As such, assistance is not always humanitarian based nor independent from the donor state's political agenda. Realpolitik asserts that every country's foreign policy agenda is based on the security of its resources and its trade market (Walker et al., 2008). Moreover, ex-colonial economic powers share the same concern about protecting their supply lines and market. By virtue of being conditional, assistance may therefore influence the recipient state's policies. International aid can also be based on strategic goals (Kilama, 2015): for example, Hoeffler and Outram (2011) argue that international donors usually direct their aid to trading partners, while Dreher et al. (2009) found that international donors usually direct their aid based on geopolitical motives and proposed that governments that are elected members of the United Nations Security Council usually receive more aid than other developing countries. Fink et al. (2011) argue that donor governments support smaller oil exporting countries that are close geographically and that usually significantly show biases "in favor of politically less aligned countries as well as toward their former colonies". Alenisa and Dollar (2000) also suggested that donor states usually have strategic biases and support former colonies and political allies. Nushiwat (2007) contends that foreign disaster response is based on political considerations. For example, US foreign humanitarian aid is based on three considerations: domestic US politics, US foreign policy, and the domestic politics of the recipient state (Drury et al., 2005; Wei et al., 2014). Wei et al. (2014) demonstrated through different case studies that foreign assistance highly depends on the public sector of the receiving state and its economy. The studies further argued that states assist affected countries that are geographically closer to them (Wei et al., 2014).

Many other debates and reasons are presented as to why states intervene in foreign disaster response. Many studies have shown that donors adapt their international aid based on the governance strategies inside the recipient state (Kilama, 2015). For example, Acht et al. (2015) argued that when recipient states have weak institutions, donors usually direct their foreign aid toward both NGOs and multilateral organizations. On the other hand, Clist et al. (2012) argued that countries that enjoy proper governance receive more aid than others. Neumayer (2003) argued that the major decisive factors in international aid allocation are the civil and political rights. Another factor that affects the donor state is the nature of the disaster (Wei et al., 2014). Drury et al. (2005) argued that from 1964 to 1995, US foreign disaster aid was mostly geared toward droughts.

News coverage by domestic media does play a great role in influencing foreign aid relief (Olsen et al., 2003; Potter and Van Belle, 2008; Wei et al., 2014). Eisensee and Strömberg's study (2007) illustrated the relationship between the effect of media channel coverage of disasters and the US government agencies' donations. They argued that coverage of disasters can be reduced in the face of a competing international event, such as the Olympic games; this affects the international coverage and hence international relief assistance. Moreover, local legislative delays from the part of the affected state also play a role. Indeed, sometimes poor disaster response, local knowledge, and incompetent disaster management affect the donation process (Haojun et al., 2011).

Many other studies were presented to understand international intervention:

1. Geographical location: Indeed, geographical locations play a crucial role in the philosophy of aid (Wei et al., 2014). Some geographers debate the so-called geographies of generosity or the practices of giving and receiving aid, focusing on the themes of (i) "caring at a distance", which grounds aid to the theories of equality and social justice; and (ii) "geographies of responsibility", which link aid to attentiveness and responsiveness that start from those who are the nearest and dearest to us but can be extended to the globalized world (Barnett and Land, 2007; Massey, 2004). Geographies of generosity can refer to the study of different aspects of care where new modes

of spatial relationships emerge and practices reveal the multiple and complex motivations for help following the occurrence of natural disasters and/or political emergencies (Barnett and Land, 2007; Carter, 2007).

2. Trade policies: Berthelemy et al. (2004), through a three-dimensional panel, studied the equity in aid criteria between donors and concluded on the importance of strengthening trade connections in distributing aid.

3. Type of international actor: Neumayer (2003a), based on an analysis of allocation of funds between development banks and the United Nations, concluded that UN agencies take into consideration both human development aspects and economic needs, while regional development banks base their decision on the economic needs of the state.

4. Peer pressure: Round and Odedokun (2004) studied the "peer pressure" effect by analyzing the total aid of donors based on their total GDP and argued that "peer pressure" provides a positive impact on the amount of aid provided by each donor.

The available literature also argues the importance of using humanitarian aid as a diplomatic tool in disaster response (Kelman, 2007; Kelman, 2012; Wei et al., 2014): as disaster diplomacy is usually restricted to settling conflicts and reaching peace (Gaillard et al., 2008). Kelman argued that "disasters have the potential for improving, worsening, or having minimal effect on diplomacy, depending on how the situation is played and what the players choose" (cited in Kelman, 2006, 227). Disaster diplomacy is best defined as disaster response that would lead to diplomatic cooperation (Ganapati et al., 2010). Indeed, literature centered on disaster diplomacy is based on linking disaster relief and response to bilateral interstate relations. In fact, the literature mentions that states that are in conflict refrain from requesting disaster relief aid from their enemies (Kelman, 2007). Studies on disaster diplomacy illustrated how in a conflicting environment disasters can catalyze conflict but not forge cooperation (Attina, 2012). However, as illustrated by Ganapati, Kelman, and Koukis (2010), in their study on post-1999 Turkish earthquakes and the collaboration between Greece and Turkey, disasters might result in long-term cooperation between conflicting states based on three conditions: (1) when the party that provides the relief effort is met by a similar gesture, (2) when both parties realize that neighbors should always assist each other during disasters, and (3) the presence of an enabling environment that might lead to long-term cooperation.

Another debate in the diplomacy chapter focuses on the motives behind the recipient state refusing foreign aid. These political reasons are rooted in the country's foreign policy and are the bases of the refusal for linking foreign aid with the improvement of diplomatic relations or the refusal of the conditions placed by the donor (Attina, 2012).

Another related school of thought supports the idea that disasters can be a means of attenuation of a conflict between two sides (Akcinaroglu, DiCicco and Radziszewski, 2011; Hollis, 2018). While conclusive research is not enough to argue that there is a direct relation between diplomacy and the positive impact of a disaster on conflict resolution (Hollis, 2018), this theory argues that disaster can play a diplomatic role in slowing down ongoing conflicts between two sides (Akcinaroglu, DiCicco and Radziszewski, 2011). Two main variables are at play here: (1) public support for international cooperation or rapprochement, which is also referred to as "mass support", and (2) type of regime (Kelman, 2006, Akcinaroglu, DiCicco and Radziszewski, 2011). In fact, Brancatti (2007) considers public support as a key factor in disaster diplomacy. During disaster response, the population can lobby the government and decision-makers toward creating peace with rivalry states. This is based on the argument that people are at the core of peacemaking and that the will of people to create is an opportunity that governments should seize, as this support will change domestic policies toward external powers (Akcinaroglu, DiCicco and Radziszewski, 2011). A nuance should be made at this stage that although people are not at the core of international cooperation, they can hinder conflict resolution and rapprochement.

The second factor is the type of regime as this factor affects the extent to which the public can lobby decision-makers. Mostly, this factor is witnessed in a country where the government is indeed accountable to its population.

This section demonstrated that state intervention in international humanitarian response is not only based on pure humanitarian reasons. Indeed, decisions to respond and the levels of response are highly contingent upon different strategic decisions and reasons which would take into account the possible negative implications of accepting foreign aid. Indeed, this part has argued that although humanitarian assistance is the basic aim of assisting in disaster response, other factors play a role in deciding on this response: diplomatic relations, political, geostrategic, economic needs and trade interests, domestic media, and governance strategies inside the affected state in addition to natural resources such as the presence of oil in the affected state.

Conclusion

This chapter has reviewed the role of the international community in disaster response and has presented the roles played by different stakeholders in disaster response whether states, diaspora, intergovernmental organizations, regional organizations, and international nongovernmental agencies.

In general, these humanitarian actors should be restricted by four principles when responding to disasters. These include humanity, impartiality, neutrality, and independence. Given these principles, the emergency relief responses of humanitarian organizations should be based on human rights, on the principle of "do no harm", and on impartiality, irrespective of economic or political purposes. However, a lot of criticism has been directed toward international aid. This chapter has demonstrated that although international humanitarian assistance should be directed toward helping individuals in emergency situations without any discrimination based on race, citizenship, or political considerations, the reality is different: international assistance and foreign aid are mainly based on strategic, political, diplomatic, and geostrategic reasons and are dominated by economic concerns. International donors, whether states or organizations, take into consideration their own benefits and agendas when responding to disasters. It is argued that in developing countries, the role of these international players is crucial for relief efforts. Indeed, when examining literature on donations from the international community, this chapter revealed that assistance is mostly based on strategic and political reasons and is dominated by economic concerns. International humanitarian organizations have their own norms and conditional procedures for the distribution of aid, which would limit the recipient governments' ability to gain political credit. Moreover, this chapter demonstrated how some international aid emphasizes the failure of the affected governments in managing disasters and how the reliance on these international donors would lead to limited commitment from the part of the affected state and weak governance of local institutions. This chapter also reviewed the role of the diaspora in disaster response. Although the latter plays a crucial role in assisting and mobilizing resources, it is usually a short-term direct response, and these donations might be misplaced due to the absence of an effective channel for response in the affected community (Naik et al., 2007). Moreover, the efficiency and effectiveness of the assistance is usually questioned since most diaspora are not experts in disaster response or do not have an objective view of the needs of the affected community and most of the resources are usually directed to one activity which signifies a lack of proper planning for disaster recovery. This chapter argued that these remittances, on some occasions, affect political accountability as they allow certain groups to rule despite their failure in proper governance in their areas of power.

References

Acht, M., Mahmoud, T. O., & Thiele, R. (2015). Corrupt governments do not receive more state-to-state aid: Governance and the delivery of foreign aid through non-state actors. *Journal of Development Economics, 114*, 20–33.

Akcinaroglu, S., DiCicco, J. M., & Radziszewski, E. (2011). Avalanches and olive branches: A multimethod analysis of disasters and peacemaking in interstate rivalries. *Political Research Quarterly, 64*(2), 260–275.

Alesina, A., & Dollar, D. (2000). Who gives foreign aid to whom and why? *Journal of Economic Growth, 5*(1), 33—63.

Annen, K., & Strickland, S. (2017). Global samaritans? Donor election cycles and the allocation of humanitarian aid. *European Economic Review, 96*, 38–47.

Attuna, F. (2012). *The politics and policies of relief, aid and reconstruction: Contrasting approaches to disasters and emergencies.* Palgrave Macmillan, London: Springer.

Balcik, B., Beamon, B. M., Krejci, C. C., Muramatsu, K. M., & Ramirez, M. (2010). Coordination in humanitarian relief chains: Practices, challenges, and opportunities. *International Journal of Production Economics, 126*(1), 22–34.

Barnett, J. (2007). Environmental security and peace. *Journal of Human Security, 3*(1), 4–16.

Barnett, C. and Land, D. (2007) 'Geographies of generosity: beyond the 'moral turn", *Geoforum, 38*(6), 1065–1075.

Beamon, B. M., & Balcik, B. (2008). Performance measurement in humanitarian relief chains. *International Journal of Public Sector Management, 21*(1), 4–25.

Bell, C. (2010). Haiti Calling, Calling Haiti: Understanding information needs and communications patterns among Haitians overseas following the quake of 12 January 2010. [Report for the Communications with Disaster Affected Populations Group] UN OCHA.

Berthélemy, J.-C., & Tichit, A. (2004). Bilateral donors' aid allocation decisions - A three-dimensional panel analysis. *International Review of Economics and Finance, 13*(253), 274.

Bostrom, A., Brown, D., Cechvala, S., & S. (2016). Humanitarian effectiveness & the role of the diaspora: A CDA literature review. CDA practical learning for international action. https://www.cdacollaborative.org/wp-content/uploads/2016/05/Humanitarian-Effectiveness-and-the-Role-of-the-Diaspora.pdf.

Brancati, D. (2007). Political aftershocks: The impact of earthquakes on intrastate conflict. *Journal of Conflict Resolution, 51*(5), 715–743.

Carter, S. (2007). 'Mobilising generosity, framing geopolitics: Narrating crisis in the homeland through diasporic media', *Geoforum, 38*(6), 1102–1112.

Clist, P., Isopi, A., & Morrissey, O. (2012). Selectivity on aid modality: Determinants of budget support from multilateral donors. *Review of International Organizations, 7*(3), 267–284.

Cook, A. D. B., Shrestha, M., & Htet, Z. B. (2018). An assessment of international emergency disaster response to the 2015 Nepal earthquakes. *International Journal of Disaster Risk Reduction, 31*, 535–547,

Coppola, D. P. (2015). Participants – Multilateral organizations and international Financial Institutions. In *Introduction to International Disaster Management* (pp. 588–680). https://doi.org/10.1016/B978-0-12-801477-6.00010-1.

Darcy, J., & Hofmann, C. A. (2003). According to Need? Needs Assessment and Decision Making in the Humanitarian sector. *HPG Report no. 15*, London.

Dreher, A., Sturm, J.-E., & Vreeland, J. (2009). Development aid and international politics: Does membership on the UN Security Council influence World Bank decisions. *Journal of Development Economics, 88*(1), 1–18.

Drury, A. C., Olson, R. S., & Van Belle, D. A. (2005). The politics of humanitarian aid: U.S. foreign disaster aid, 1964–1995. *Journal of Politics, 67*(2), 454–473.

Eisensee, T., & Stromberg, D. (2007). News floods, news droughts, and U.S. disaster relief. *Quarterly Journal of Economics, 122*(2), 693–728.

Fagen, P. (2006). *Remittances in crises: A Haiti case study.* [HPG Background Paper] London: Humanitarian Policy Group, ODI, April.

Fink, G., & Redaelli, S. (2011). Determinants of international emergency aid - Humanitarian need only? *World Development, 39*(5), 741–757.

Gaillard, J.-C., Clave, E., & Kelman, I. (2008). Wave of peace? Tsunami disaster diplomacy in Aceh, Indonesia. *Geoforum, 39*(1), 511–526.

Ganapati, N. E., Kelman, I., & Koukis, T. (2010). Analyzing Greek-Turkish disaster-related cooperation: A disaster diplomacy perspective. *Cooperation and Conflict, 45*(2), 162–185.

Godfrey, M., Sophal, C., Kato, T. A., Vou Piseth, L., Dorina, P., Saravy, T., … Sovannarith, S. (2002). Technical assistance and capacity development in an aid-dependent economy: The experience of Cambodia. *World Development, 30*(3), 355–373.

Hammond, L., et al. (2011). Cash and compassion: The role of the Somali diaspora in relief, development and Peacebuilding. UNDP. Accessed 25 July 2014: http://www.refworld.org/docid/4f61b12d2.html.

Hannigan, J. (2012). *Disasters without borders: The international politics of natural disasters.* Cambridge: Polity Press.

Haojun, F., Jianqi, S.and Shike, H. (2011) 'Retrospective, analytical study of field first aid following the Wenchuan Earthquake in China', *Prehospital and Disaster Medicine, 26*(2), 130–134.

Hoeffler, A., & Outram, V. (2011). Need, merit, or self-interest: What determines the allocation of aid? *Review of Development Economics, 15*(2), 237–250.

Hollis, S. (2015). *The role of regional organizations in disaster risk management.* Basingstoke: Palgrave Macmillan.

Hollis, S. (2018). Bridging international relations and disaster studies: The case of disaster–conflict scholarship. *Disasters, 42*(1), 19–40.

IFRC. (2003). *World disasters report 2003.* Geneva: International Federation of Red Cross and Red Crescent Societies.

IFRC. (2021). *Strategy 2030.* Geneva: International Federation of Red Cross and Red Crescent Societies.

Jones, S., Katie, J., Oven, b., & Aryal, K. (2014). Governance struggles and policy processes in disaster risk reduction: A case study from Nepal. *Geoforum, 57*, 78–90.

Kelman, I. (2006). Acting on disaster diplomacy. *Journal of International Affairs, 59*(2), 215–240.

Kelman, I. (2007). Hurricane Katrina disaster diplomacy. *Disasters, 31*(3), 288–309.

Kelman, I. (2012). *Disaster diplomacy: How disasters affect peace and conflict.* Abingdon, UK: Routledge.

Kilama, E. (2015). Evidence on donors competition in Africa: Traditional donors versus China. *Journal of International Development, 28*(4), 528–551.

King, D., & Grullon, H. (2013). Diaspora communities as aid providers. [Online Article]. *International Organization for Migration.* August-September. https://www.iom.int/cms/en/sites/iom/home/what-we-do/migration-policy-and -research /migration-policy-1/migration-policy-practice/issues/augustseptem ber-2013/diaspora-co mmunities-as-aid-prov.html.

Kleist, N., & Vammen, I. (2012). Diaspora groups and development in fragile situations: Lessons learnt. [DIIS report 2012, 09]. Copenhagen: Danish Institute for International Studies.

Kova´cs, G., & Spens, K. (2008). Chapter 13. Humanitarian logistics revisited. In J. S. Arlbjørn, A. Halldo´rsson, M. Jahre & K. Spens (Eds.), *Northern lights in logistics and supply chain management* (pp. 217–232). Copenhagen: CBS Press.

Lindley, A. (2006). *Migrant remittances in the context of crisis in Somali society: A case study of Hargeisa.* [HPG Background Paper] London: Humanitarian Policy Group, ODI, April.

Massey, D. (2004) 'Geographies of responsibility', *Geografiska Annaler: Series B, Human Geography, 86*(1), 5–18.

Meier, P. (2011). New information technologies and their impact on the humanitarian sector. *International Review of the Red Cross, 93*(884), 1239–1263.

Meier, P. (2013). Crisis maps." In *McKinsey on society's Voices on Society Vol. 5: The Art and Science of Delivery.* Skoll World Forum on Social Entrepreneurship. Accessed 6 August 2014: http://voices.mckinseyonsociety.com/crisis-maps/.

Moore, S., Eng, E., & Daniel, M. (2003). International NGOs and the role of network centrality in humanitarian aid operations: A case study of coordination during the 2000 Mozambique floods. *Disasters, 27*(4), 305–318.

Morgenthau, H. (1978). *Politics among nations: The struggle for power and peace.* New York: Alfred A. Knopf.

Naik, A., Stigter, E., & Laczko, F. (2007). *Diaspora response to natural disasters in migration, development and natural disasters.* IOM Migration Research Series. United Nations. https://doi.org/10.18356/3e4d8d6d-en.

Neumayer, E. (2003). Do human rights matter in bilateral aid allocation? A quantitative analysis of 21 donor countries. *Social Science Quarterly, 84*(3), 650–666.

Neumayer, E. (2003a). The determinants of aid allocation by regional multilateral development banks and United Nations agencies. *International Studies Quarterly, 47*(1), 101–122.

Nishimoto, K. (2014). The role of international organizations in disaster response: A case study of recent earthquakes in Japan. In D. Caron, M. Kelly & A. Telesetsky (Eds.), *The international law of disaster relief* (pp. 295–313). Cambridge: Cambridge University Press. https://doi.org/10.1017/CBO9781107447844.023.

Nushiwat, M. (2007). Foreign aid to developing countries: Does it crowd-out the recipient countries' domestic savings? *International Research Journal of Finance and Economics, 11*, 94–102.

Okuwaki, N. (2006). Natural disasters and international cooperation – Hyogo declaration and the contribution of Japan. *Juristo, 1321*, 66–72.

Olsen, G. R., Carstensen, N., & Høyen, K. (2003). Humanitarian crises: What determines the level of emergency assistance? Media coverage, donor interests and the aid business. *Disasters, 27*(2), 109–126.

Olson, R. S., & Gawronski, V. T. (2010). From disaster event to political crisis: A "5C+A" framework for analysis. *International Studies Perspectives, 11*(3), 205–221.

Potter, D. M., & Van Belle, D. (2008). News coverage and Japanese foreign disaster aid: A comparative example of bureaucratic responsiveness to the news media. *International Relations of the Asia-Pacific, 9*(2), 295–315.

Rajan, S. R. (2002). Disaster, development, and governance: Reflections on the lessons of Bhopal. *Environmental Values, 11*(3), 369–394.

Round, J., & Odedokun, M. (2004). Aid effort and its determinants. *International Review of Economics and Finance, 13*(3), 293—309.

Sahloul, Z. (2014). "The humanitarian crisis in Syria: Views from the ground". Testimony to the house foreign relations committee, subcommittee on the Middle East and North Africa. Washington, DC: U.S. Congress, 21 May. Accessed 24 September 2014: http://docs.house.gov/meetings/FA/FA13/20140521 /102243/HHRG-113-FA13-Wstate- SahloulZ-20140521.pdf.

Sida. (2014). Our work in Somalia. Stockholm: Swedish International Development Cooperation. Accessed 8 September 2014: http://www.sida.se/English/where we- work/Africa/Somalia/Our-work-in-Somalia/.

Steets, J., Reichhold, U., & Sagmeister, E. (2012). Evaluation and review of humanitarian access strategies in DG ECHO funded interventions. Berlin: Global Public Policy Institute, 29 June. Accessed 8 September 2014: http://ec .europa.eu/echo/files/evaluation/2012/GPPi_Access-Report.pdf.

Telec, A. (2014). Challenges to state sovereignty in the provision of international natural disaster relief. In D. Caron, M. Kelly & A. Telesetsky (Eds.), *The international law of disaster relief* (pp. 270–292). Cambridge: Cambridge University Press. https://doi.orgt/10.1017/CBO9781107447844.021.

Van Hear, N., Pieke, F., & Vertovec, S. (2004). The contribution of UK-based diasporas to development and poverty reduction. ESRC Centre on Migration, Policy and society (COMPAS), University of Oxford. Accessed 22 August 2014: http://www.compas.ox.ac.uk/fileadmin/files/Publications/Reports/DFID %20diaspora%20report.pdf.

Walker, P., & Maxwell, D. (2008). *Shaping the humanitarian world*. London: Routledge.

Walker, P., Wisner, B., Leaning, J., & Minear, L. (2005). Smoke and mirrors: Deficiencies in disaster funding. *British Medical Journal, 330*(7485), 247–250.

Watson, S. D. (2019). *International order and the politics of disaster* (1st ed.). New York: Routledge.

Weber, C. (2010). *International relations theory: A critical introduction*. London: Routledge.

Wei, J., & Marinova, D. (2016). The orientation of disaster donations: Differences in the global response to five major earthquakes. *Disasters, 40*(3), 452–475.

Wei, J., Marinova, D., & Zhao, D. (2014). Disaster assistance: Determinants of countries around the world contributing towards disaster donations. *International Journal of Emergency Management, 10*(1), 48–66.

Wei, J., Wang, A., & Wang, F. (2019). Humanitarian organizations in international disaster relief: Understanding the linkage between donors and recipient countries. *Voluntas, 30*(6), 1212–1228. https://doi.org/ezproxy.aub.edu.lb/10.1007/s11266 -019-00172-x.

Zagefka, H., & James, T. (2015). The psychology of charitable donations to disaster victims and beyond. *Social Issues and Policy Review, 9*(1), 155–192.

Zhang, J. (2006). Public diplomacy as symbolic interactions: A case study of Asian tsunami relief campaigns. *Public Relations Review, 32*(1), 26–32.

2 Local Players in Disaster Response

Introduction

When disasters strike, the first to respond are local players. Since disasters cause complex situations, emergency responses should also include different players such as state and nonstate actors in addition to private organizations. Indeed, in disaster management, proper governance during emergency responses is affected by the interplay of power between these different actors who often have unequal access to resources (Ojha et al., 2009). Governance is both a descriptive and a normative term (Renn et al., 2011). From a descriptive viewpoint, it "refers to the complex web of manifold interactions between heterogeneous actors pertaining to a particular policy domain" (Jones et al., 2014, p. 79 and see Renn et al., 2011). From a normative perspective, good governance encompasses different actors, including the state working on developing positive changes in society through public sector reforms and projects based on the principles of accountability, coherence, social justice, and participation (Jones et al., 2014; Renn et al., 2011; Ahrens & Rudolph, 2006; Lebel et al., 2006). In disaster management, good governance plays a crucial role and entails

> the adoption and promotion of robust and sound policies, legislation, coordination mechanisms and regulatory frameworks, and the creation of an enabling environment that is characterized by appropriate decision-making processes to allow effective participation of stakeholders, complemented by the appropriate allocation of resources. (Jones et al., 2014; WMO, 2012)

Considering the above, this chapter will review the role of local actors in disaster response in a developing context and how the interplay between different actors affects disaster response. The first section, "Setting the Theoretical Context", will put this relationship in its theoretical context by

DOI: 10.4324/9781003222545-3

reviewing the literature and conceptual frameworks of government–nonprofit relationships in a developed and developing context. It will further explore the different negative and positive aspects of such a relationship by aligning these frameworks with the five dimensions of collaboration described by Thomson, Perry, and Miller (2007) and Curnin and O'Hara (2019).

The second section, "Disaster Management Coordination, Cooperation, and the Concept of Trust between Different Players", will discuss the importance of building trust between organizations involved in emergency relief services to secure a proper response. The third section, "Disaster Response, Developing Context, and Public Sector Corruption", will review the theories on disaster response in developing context and the link between corruption and disaster response. The fourth section, "Role of the National State, Local State, and the Military", will review the role of the state and local government and the national army with an emphasis on developing context and will review the role of nonstate actors, including communities, volunteers, and nongovernmental agencies; the fifth section, "Community and Disaster Response", reviews the role of the community and disaster response. The main aim of this chapter is to analyze the role of different local players in disaster management and understand the relationship that develops between these different players. It analyzes the interplay of power and knowledge among different actors and how the uneven power balances lead to the development of new governance approaches to disaster response.

Setting the Theoretical Context

Since governance requires different players working together for an effective decision-making process, it is crucial to review the theories that characterize state–nonstate actors. Indeed, there is long-standing literature that discusses state–nonprofit relationships (Salamon & Anheier, 1998; Young, 1999; Najam, 2000; Young, 2000; Marchetti, 2018; Haddad, 2017). Salamon and Anheier (1998) argued that "civil society is rooted in the social, political, and economic status of the society and the economic and political regimes are the ones regulating the government–civil society relationship" (Kövér, 2021).

The factors determining this relationship are autonomy (Read, 2008), partnership (participation) (Gaventa, 2006, Sørvoll & Bengtsson, 2019), and solidarity, both inward and outward (Kövér, 2021).

(1) Autonomy: Autonomy is viewed as civil society's ability to protect itself from both state and market (Cohen & Arato, 1997). Indeed, this autonomy is crucial to protect civil society from government power

(Tocqueville, 2000) and economic power (Cohen & Arato, 1997). It is based on balancing the autonomy of civil society from the state and the market based on trust and reciprocity (Della Porta, 2020). This autonomy is affected by the type of regime under which it operates: in authoritarian ones, organizations are under a top-down model of control, while in democratic countries where state and civil society are cooperating and collaborating, dependency on resources sometimes affects the autonomy of the organizations. However, in the communitarian conception, the state's role is seen as central and its influence on organizations is not viewed as an infringement (Walzer, 1998).

(2) Partnership: Partnership in this context is based on power sharing over decisions. It is grounded in collaboration among actors and refers to participatory democracy. It is based on the shift from government to governance (Kövér, 2021). Through this partnership, citizens participate in the development of the policies that are based on the needs of the community (Kövér, 2021). These partnerships are important since they "allow for a widening of democracy, it is necessary to reform the state and government to make them act in partnership with civil society" (Mouffe, 2005, p. 58).

(3) Solidarity: Inward solidarity in this context is mainly the cohesive bond that holds all members of the organization together: it includes sectoral solidarity where the collective goals of the organizations surpass the interests of the individual organization (Sørvoll & Bengtsson, 2019). Outward solidarity, on the other hand, is based on associations that influence public policy through advocacy and campaigns (Sørvoll & Bengtsson, 2019). In this context, civil society opposes an authoritarian state, and citizens pressure the system for change leading to democracy from below (Foley & Edwards, 1996, p. 46).

Klein and Lee (2019) argue that studies and analysis of the relationship between government and civil society are limited to the politics of this influence and cannot truly portray the complexity of such a relationship. Pauly, De Rynck, and Verschuere (2016) analyzed this relationship from the neo-Gramscian perspective by looking at the transition from government to participatory governance. Taking the social theory as a basis, Riley and Fernández (2014) compared the bottom-up and the top-down approaches in addition to the heteronomous and the autonomous civil society in the context of totalitarian and authoritarian regimes. Klein and Lee (2019) argued that the infiltration theory reaffirms that the main feature of civil society is interdependence, as the boundaries of the three different players (government, NGOs, and the market) are blurred. This theory discusses the dynamics of civil society – government and economic actors. The authors criticized "the domain-focused accounts of the politics of civil society" where the focal point is preserving the autonomy of civil society from the interference of the state and economic actors (Kövér, 2021). They further argue that this infiltration is inevitable. Grønbjerg and Smith (2021), on the other hand, stated that the relationship between civil society, government, market, and informal (household) actors changes across the domains. Conceptual frameworks addressing this relationship have evolved throughout history (Haddad, 2017, 2018). While in the 1980s this relationship was mainly viewed as unidimensional, NGOs are filling the gap left by the state through social services (Salamon, 1995; Young, 1999; Haddad, 2017); in 1991, Clark argued that this relationship is based on NGOs having the choice of opposing, complementing, or reforming the state (Clark, 1991). In 1992, Gidron et al. argued that NGO–government relationship is based on four typologies: government is dominant, NGOs are dominant, dual relationship, or collaboration.

Coston (1998) presented an eight-level taxonomy to define this relationship and argued that this relationship varies based on the organization, the government agency, and the policy area (Coston, 1998). Thus, analyzing this relationship is based on the role played by the state (Brinkerhoff & Brinkerhoff, 2002). It was not until 2000 that this relationship was viewed from the perspectives of both actors: indeed, Young (2000) argued that this relationship can be either supplementary, complementary, or adversarial. Najam (2000) argued that this relationship should be based on both government initiative and the interest of both actors, and argued that this relationship is based on four different types: confrontation, cooperation, complementary, and co-optation.

Marchetti and Tocci (2009) presented a framework for analyzing this relationship in conflict and post-conflict societies. They argued that the state would directly affect and shape the role of civil society. In this regard, they developed four different contextual categories to better understand the circumstances in which civil society functions, which directly affect the nature of these associations. These are (1) failing or failed state context; (2) the nature of the state in question: in this regard we look at the level of democracy, the openness of the regime, the legal framework, and the freedom of associations; (3) the socioeconomic nature of the state: mainly developed or underdeveloped; and (4) the nature and the role of the international community. All these factors would affect and shape the nature of the civil society (Haddad, 2018).

In disaster response and recovery, government–nonprofit relation is a complex phenomenon. Many frameworks were introduced to analyze these state–nonprofit relationships. Thomson et al. (2007) presented a multidimensional framework of collaboration based on five components: (1)

administration or the management of the operation, (2) norms that involve interaction between partners that establish a trustworthy relationship, (3) governance or the presence of an organizational structure that would create the right environment to resolve problems, (4) mutuality or the shared interest between the different actors, and (5) autonomy or the ability of the organization to keep its own identity. Expanding on the work of Thomson et al. (2007), Currin and Ohara (2019) argued that three characteristics are required in disaster recovery: (1) interorganizational structures, (2) trust in the relationship, and (3) role clarity. Based on Currin and Ohara (2019), the latter is crucial to enable the first two characteristics as role clarity builds trust and at the same time enhances collaboration in the recovery phase.

This section has analyzed theories that govern state–nonprofit relationships and reviewed the different theories and conceptual frameworks to understand the government–civil society relationship. It is also argued that there are three different factors that determine this relationship: autonomy, partnership (participation), and solidarity (inward and outward). It further reviewed the conceptual framework governing this relationship during and post-disasters. Since trust is a major player in disaster response, the next section will expand on the importance of building mutual trust between the different players as a way to achieve success in disaster response and recovery. It further reviews the complex relationship that appears during disaster response and the importance of cooperation and coordination.

Disaster Management Coordination, Cooperation, and the Concept of Trust between Different Players

Literature on disaster management stresses the importance of building trust between stakeholders for a successful disaster response. This trust among institutions was first discussed by Almond and Verba in 1965 and Inglehart (1990), who discussed the importance of trust in the functioning of democratic rule. Indeed, the concept of trust is viewed as a tool to assess the legitimacy of public institutions (Malesic, 2019). When disaster strikes, as Kervyn et al. (2014) stated, political trust plays a great role in the expectation of the public in both the mitigation and intervention programs. If a public institution or an organization has a poor reputation and is not trusted, then the cooperation of the population with the latter in the disaster response efforts will be highly difficult (Malesic, 2019).

In disaster response and risk management, trust in institutions is defined by Löfstedt (2005) as "an acceptance of decisions by the constituents without questioning the rationale behind them" (p.48). Cvetkovich and Löfstedt (1999) argued that this trust in institutions in disaster management is based on understanding the public institutional goals, motives, and actions in addition to their values. When it comes to factors that influence this trust in public institutions, many theories are presented: social capital theory, media coverage theory, motivational theory, and performance theory (Malesic, 2018; Hardin, 1999; Warren, 1999; Putnam, 2001).

Performance theory argues that trust in institutions is based on the performance of institutions. Based on Mishler and Rose (2001), institutions that perform well publicly generate trust, while others that underperform mirror distrust. Thus, performance is crucial in building trust with citizens. By extension, Malesic (2019, p. 604) argued that "an institution (e.g., local government) that depends on the cooperation of the population for its disaster response efforts will have difficulties mobilizing the public if it is perceived to have a poor reputation and is not well trusted". In disaster response, when it comes to trust in the government and other public institutions, Liang (2016) and Thoresen et al. (2018) argued that in post-disaster, the level of trust in public institutions decreases, and this trust also differs between the survivors and the general population: "the levels of institutional trust in the police and judicial system were notably lower in survivors and the bereaved than in the general population" (Thoresen. et al., 2018, p. 605). In contrast, Schupp et al. (2017) argued the opposite: in their study, they concluded that post-disaster survivors trusted the police and civil servants more than they did previously.

In his study on disaster response and trust, Malesic (2019) argued that there is a positive correlation between public trust in the government and the public perception of government performance during disaster. Malesic (2019) concluded that while trust in government is usually low, it tends to increase during disasters. He also concluded that civil defense institutions and employees, such as firemen, in addition to the military and NGOs, are highly trusted both before and during disasters. Conversely, institutions, such as local government that will need the cooperation of its citizens in disaster response, will face difficulties in attracting assistance if they suffer from a bad reputation and a lack of trust. Thus, Kervyn et al. (2014, p. 271) argued that in post-disaster, "political trust impacts an organization's reputation and concurrently affects the public's expectation of the organization's mitigation and intervention efforts".

Malesic (2019) identified three main types of trust: social, political, and institutional. Social trust is viewed as encompassing social institutions and organizations in addition to trust among individuals, groups, and organizations in the society. This type of trust appears when disaster victims and the whole community interact with disaster managers. On the other hand, slow response would lead to dissatisfaction and in low social trust (Kang & Skidmore, 2018). Political trust is viewed as trust in the government and the bureaucracies in addition to trust in the political and professional organizations responsible for disaster response. White and Fu (2012) defined political trust as "the positive appraisal by citizens of their government and institutions", whereas the latter represents "a broader idea that others in society will act in accordance with values, such as honesty and fairness, which make relationships between individuals worthwhile". Institutional trust is defined as "a favorable attitude of the public towards institutions that are not political, e.g., disaster response institutions" (Malesic, 2019). Malesic (2019) also argues that these different types of trust complement and overlap with each other; hence, it is crucial to have trust in authority and institutions as well as establish a credible social context. As such, the level of trust is based on the pace of government response and concurrently on the support of the community. To come up with a successful disaster response strategy, there is a need to build trust between the different players in disaster management, including public institutions and the government, disaster survivors, and nonstate actors.

Coordination, Cooperation, and Collaboration in Disaster Response

Building on the concept of trust, another strain of literature focuses on the role of networking and building networks in times of crisis (Goodin & Robinson, 2020). During a crisis, there is a need to create a network of response that would engage administrative agencies with the private sectors (Goodin & Robinson, 2020).

Coordination and cooperation in disaster response are directly connected to a greater debate on the roles of the state, the private sector, and nongovernmental organizations in ensuring collective security (Mizan & Fuadi, 2016). Coordination implies different organizations working together, sharing information and resources to achieve a common goal (Bardach, 1998; Yeo & Comfort, 2017). Collaboration, on the other hand, in disaster response has had a different definition: it is viewed as a partnership process between different organizations to work closely to implement their operations (Cao & Zhang, 2011; Simatupang & Sridharan, 2002). It takes place when different players from different organizations decide to initiate and sustain a relationship based on trust and share ownership of collective objectives (FEMA, 2007; Kamensky & Burlin, 2004). This is indispensable to deal with uncertainty and complex extreme events (Arklay, 2015; Waugh & Streib, 2006). It is a process where different actors work together through creating clear rules and structures (Mushtari & Gonçalves, 2017). It goes at a higher level than cooperation and coordination (Mushtari & Gonçalves, 2017). While at the cooperation level different players share information for good intentions (Mushtari & Gonçalves, 2017), at the coordination level, activities and resources are shared across sectors (Mushtari & Gonçalves, 2017); at the collaboration level, power, capabilities, activities, and resources are shared. For any disaster response to be effective and ensure that adequate measures are in place, interorganizational collaboration is necessary (Mushtari & Gonçalves, 2017), especially since disasters would overwhelm the resources of the governments involved (Waugh, 2007); Yeo and Comfort (2017) further stressed on the importance of coordination among agencies and organizations for effective disaster response. Thus, different sectors need to collaborate whether they are public, for profit and nonprofit. Roberts (2010) also argued that disaster response needs a network that links federal, state, and local governments with private for-profit and nonprofit organizations with a clear hierarchy of command from above and with broad agreements of shared goals and responsibilities (Bisri & Fuady, 2016).

Based on the importance and role of the nonprofit organizations in responding to disaster, there has been a raised interest in analyzing the role of these organizations and how they collaborate with the public sector and the ideal ways to overcome barriers that might affect such collaboration (Hermansson, 2016; Nolte, 2018). Martin et al. (2016) argued that the success of collaboration in disaster response was based on preexisting interactions prior to the disaster. Heaslip et al. (2012) and Nurmala et al. (2017) argued that the key practices for humanitarian actors are communication/information diffusion, coordination, collaboration/partnering, and cooperation.

In analyzing the 9/11 response, Kapucu (2006) argued that despite the absence of clear roadmaps and structure, nonprofit sectors replied in an efficient manner. However, the study did not demonstrate the time frame that these organizations worked within, without clear roadmaps and when the government realized that these organizations should be included in existing interorganizational structures (Curnin & O'Hara, 2019). In analyzing Hurricane Katrina, Butts et al. (2012) stressed on the interorganizational collaboration in the nonprofit and public sectors, mainly the American Red Cross in the response process. Simo and Bies (2007) also stressed on the role of the nonprofit sector in responding to Hurricane Katrina in the wake of the overwhelming failures of public administration particularly considering the absence of adequate service provision. Nolte, Martin, and Boenigk (2012) identified the importance of administrative mechanisms to allow nonprofit organizations to participate in the coordination process in disaster response; they also stressed on interorganizational relationships as important mechanisms for response. Robinson, Berrett, and Stone (2006), by studying the response to Hurricane Katrina, also stressed on the importance of well-established and coherent administrative arrangements as well the importance of communication and collaboration with the nonprofit organizations.

Nolte, Martin, and Boenigk (2012) also stressed the need for administrative mechanisms to allow nonprofit organizations to participate in the broader network of coordination arrangements and clearly defined interorganizational structures to facilitate interorganizational collaboration in disasters.

Disaster Response, Developing Context, and Public Sector Corruption

It is important to examine the relationship between naturally occurring or man-made disasters and public sector corruption, to bridge the gap in approaches to disaster response and ensure that resources are utilized first and foremost for the benefit of affected populations. It is also important to examine the relationship both ways, in terms of the impact of corruption on disaster response, as well as the impact of disaster relief on corruption to have a more nuanced image of government-led disaster response.

Most studies have focused on the country's ability to counter the negative effects of disaster. Different studies have shown that countries that have a high level of per capita income encounter a lower number of deaths during disasters (Kahn, 2005; Skidmore & Toya, 2002; Noy, 2009; Anbarci, Escaleras, and Register, 2005). Studies have also indicated that the more developed the financial system in the state and the greater the openness to trade, the more the state is protected from disaster (Toya & Skidmore, 2007). While literature on disaster management also argues that the level of destruction caused by natural disasters are mitigated by the institutions of the country, recent studies have argued that corruption in the public sector and natural disaster are related (Escaleras, Anbarci, & Register, 2007). Indeed, corrupt states are affected the most in the time of natural disaster, especially in the number of deaths and the level of destruction, as compared to less corrupt countries (Leeson & Sobel, 2008).

Escaleras and Register (2016) assess the correlation between public sector corruption and natural disasters, showing that public sector corruption increases the number of deaths and the extent of the damage caused by natural disasters. Distinguishing between natural disasters and natural hazards, the authors further demonstrate, using several examples, that the probability of hazards escalating to disasters often corresponds to corruption levels. Escaleras and Register (2016) interestingly point out that even when it comes to naturally occurring disasters, a link can be made between the probability of these disasters occurring and humanity's footprint, which is made worse by a corrupt public sector that does not prioritize environmental conservation.

Similarly, the occurrence of these disasters increases public sector corruption. The appeal of receiving funding can make predisposed public officials more corruptible and having access to funds can lead corrupt individuals in government to engage in corrupt or dishonest practices (Escaleras & Register, 2016). Citing certain cases, the authors contend that a large portion of the death and destruction caused by natural disasters is comparatively avoidable. This means that an absence of corruption would minimize the fatalities and tangible consequences of the disaster. In their analysis of earthquakes at the intersection of disaster response and public sector corruption, Escaleras et al. (2007) examine the deadly consequences of corruption in the aftermath of disasters, which could be the result of practices in which aid and funding, local or international, are misused by officials.

By extension, the authors illustrate the correlation between public sector corruption and deaths resulting from natural disasters by referring to earthquakes as a primary example (Escaleras et al., 2007). In their analysis of poor development decisions stemming from corruption, Escaleras et al. (2007) state that "the marriage of corrupt contractors and corrupt building inspectors and other public officials resulted in ignored building codes, lax enforcement and the absence of on-site inspection, which is deadly when it occurs in earthquake-prone areas" (p. 210). To counter this issue, Green (2005) argues for a different perspective on natural disasters which focuses on the role played by states in exacerbating the outcomes of these natural disasters, through decision-making and fraudulent practices. The author therefore argues for a new approach to natural disasters, namely: for their classification as human rights violations often caused by corrupt public sector practices (Green, 2005).

It is important to consider the economic background within which disasters occur, and Green (2005) establishes a positive correlation between a liberal free-market economy and substantial, avoidable damage incurred by natural disasters. Free-market economies are based on the privatization of public, often unsuitable, or undeveloped land, for private and sometimes residential construction (Green, 2005). According to Green (2005), this is made easier by corrupt public sector officials overlooking regulations due to their vested interests in certain projects, due to negligence, or to gain the industry's support and funding in upcoming elections, ultimately making the consequences of natural disasters and the number of resulting deaths more dire. The author also points to the negative impact of clientelism, for instance irresponsible construction permissions being granted by appointed individuals in local municipalities who are unqualified or prone to bribery (Green, 2005). This also becomes an issue in the rescue efforts and disaster-aftermath decision-making process as those making the decisions may be unfit for their positions and lack the necessary expertise (Green, 2005).

Shughart (2011) presents the argument that disaster relief is unfavorable when provided as a public good in part due to preexisting corruption in the public sector, as well as the increased potential for corruption in the aftermath of disasters. The author specifically cites examples such as governments providing incentives for citizens residing in disaster-prone areas, which leads to a higher number of deaths in the event of a disaster (Shughart, 2011). The author also argues that government-based relief, which according to the study tends to be unequal, insufficient, and in many cases exclusionary, limits or holds back other, more effective sources of funding which could arise in its absence (Shughart, 2011).

The literature also suggested a clear relationship between state structure and disaster response. In this regard, Noy (2009) concluded that the death rate resulting from disasters is affected by the rates of literacy, size of the government, and openness to international trade: "these results suggest that the destructive potential of natural disasters can to some extent be mitigated (or exaggerated) by a country's institutions". In addition, Escaleras (2105) suggested four general categories of determinants: (1) economic factors, (2) political structure and environment, (3) social factors, and (4) historical factors.

Yamamura (2014) provides useful insights by studying the link between natural disasters and corruption comparatively in developed and developing countries. The study finds that natural disasters lead to a rise in corruption in both developing and developed countries; however, there is a greater increase in the levels of public sector corruption in developed countries in the aftermath of disasters. In line with the Escaleras et al. argument, Yamamura (2014) highlights cases in which relief funds were allocated for different purposes by politicians seeking to gain popularity for an upcoming election and secure their voter base. The author also sheds light on how public sector corruption increases with the severity of the damage caused as well as the frequency of natural disasters (Yamamura, 2014). This means that the more destruction and casualties that a disaster yields, and the more likely it is for disasters to reoccur, the more likely it will be for public sector corruption to increase as a result.

To put the link between corruption and disasters into context, Kratcoski (2018) highlights that the occurrence of disasters often presents decision-makers with an opportunity to maximize their personal gain or advance their interests by engaging in corrupt practices in the direct response period, as well as in the allocation of resources and funds in the period following the disaster. This affects rescue processes as well as relief and reconstruction efforts Kratcoski (2018) further points out that crises and disasters are easily exploited by black market beneficiaries, for instance by influencing local currency rates to gain a financial advantage.

Calossi et al. (2012) reaffirm that the extent of the damage caused by disasters is directly associated with the levels of public sector corruption, as well as the potential for disasters to provide opportunities for corruption. The authors also shed light on the importance of considering existing levels of corruption and how they will affect the allocation of relief funds negatively (Calossi et al., 2012). As part of the solution to this issue, the authors contend that international treaties tackling corruption would be beneficial if implemented and adjusted to post-disaster contexts by NGOs and civil society actors (Calossi et al., 2012).

Throughout their study, Nikolova and Marinov (2017) demonstrate that unexpected large financial influxes, referred to as windfalls, lead to higher levels of corruption in the public sector, mainly using examples from cases of flood-related disasters. According to Nikolova and Marinov (2017), these financial windfalls, mainly in the form of international relief funds, increase corruption levels even in developed countries at several levels, from local municipalities to higher-level government officials at the state level. The research conducted shows that the allocation of funds is determined by political accountability, upheld either by popular support and electability or by judicial measures in case a strong judicial system was present (Nikolova & Marinov, 2017). The study also showed that more corrupt public officials tend to resign or halt their political careers after their term ends, expecting that they've lost popular support and would no longer succeed in elections due to the disaster (Nikolova & Marinov, 2017).

Role of the National State, Local State, and the Military

The third strand of literature focuses on the major role played by the state actors, and as such, this section will review the role played by the national, state, local, and municipal governments in addition to the role assumed by the army in both developed and developing contexts.

Role of the State

While the trend toward governing beyond the state and nonstate actors are the ones stepping in to fill the gap in responding to disasters (Bulkeley et al., 2012), the role of state remains crucial as it is considered the "center of considerable political power" (Pierre & Peters, 2000, p. 12).

Maxwell and Walker (2008) reviewed the historical response of the state and argued that the role of the state in disaster response goes back to the 23rd century BCE. Since then, the role of both central and local governments in disaster management has become more crucial (Christoplos et al., 2001). This role of the government was also stressed upon in different resolutions and international conventions.

To name a few, the UN General Assembly resolution 46/182 identified the relationship of each actor in disaster response: mainly the role of state and its responsibilities. Based on this resolution, the sovereignty, integrity, and national unity of the state should be respected based on the Charter of the United Nations, and as such any humanitarian assistance should be based on the consent of the affected states. Moreover, based on this resolution, the state has the responsibility to take care of the population affected by the disaster, and the main function of the state is to "initiate, organize, coordinate and execute humanitarian assistance in its territory".

According to the key UN humanitarian resolution, Resolution 46/182 of 1991:

> Each State has the responsibility first and foremost to take care of the victims of natural disasters and other emergencies occurring on its territory. Hence, the affected State has the primary role in the initiation, organization, coordination, and implementation of humanitarian assistance within its territory.

An official disaster response operation is temporary and considered official when it is established as part of the national system for civil protection and preparedness. This operation usually has a clear organizational structure, and is governed by laws and regulations (Johansson, 2018). It includes many actors who collaborate to respond to disasters (Kvarnlof & Johansson, 2014; Johansson, 2018). Structures of government entities responsible for managing the disasters vary: in some countries the responsibility is in the hands of one disaster unit that can or cannot be attached to a particular ministry or might directly report to the office of the prime minister or president (Harvey, 2009). However, more recently, the trend has moved from "standalone" disaster management offices to complex integrated legislative systems coordinating actions through sectors, departments, and ministries (Harvey, 2009). Irrespective of the structure of the disaster management units, the literature distinguishes four major responsibilities of the state: (1) declaring the state of emergency, (2) assisting and protecting the population, (3) monitoring and coordinating assistance, and (4) ensuring the functioning of an adequate normative framework (Harvey, 2009).

Declare State of Emergency

The legitimate authority should declare a state of emergency as per its internal legislative framework. When the state views that the needs exceed the capacity of the state to respond, then a state of emergency is declared. It is important to note that the state should issue the request for assistance, especially at the international level, as international actors cannot act without any official request for assistance. UN Resolution 46/182 ("Strengthening of the coordination of humanitarian emergency assistance of the United Nations", which was approved in 1991), states that:

> The sovereignty, territorial integrity and national unity of States must be fully respected in accordance with the Charter of the United Nations. In this context, humanitarian assistance should be provided with the consent of the affected country and in principle based on an appeal by the affected country.

Assist and Protect Its Population

O'Callaghan and Pantuliano (2007) argue that the fundamental responsibility of the state is to ensure the safety and security of its citizens, and to assist and protect the affected population. This physical and legal protection is the basis of sovereignty over the state's territory. In addition to being responsible for the protection of international aid workers, governments are the major entity that will be held accountable under humanitarian law since they have the coercive power to enforce laws and regulations (Harvey, 2009). Agencies of the government, such as state ministries and key line ministries responsible for health and water, or ministries responsible for disaster risk management, should also be responsible for organizing evacuation and providing food security, shelter, and healthcare (Harvey, 2009).

Monitor and Coordinate

The state is responsible for coordinating between national actors and international actors. The most important issue is to ensure timely assistance for the impacted community. Based on the IFRC's

> Guidelines for the domestic facilitation and regulation of international disaster relief and initial recovery assistance' (IDRL), affected States have the sovereign right to coordinate, regulate and monitor, disaster relief and recovery assistance provided by assisting actors on their territory, consistent with international law. (IFRC, 2007b)

In this regard, many states have introduced legislation to formalize the coordination role (Harvey, 2009).

Functioning of Normative Action

The state is responsible for promoting and adopting an international framework such as the Hyogo Framework of Action. These frameworks would facilitate international assistance and the development of a holistic view of mitigation (Harvey, 2009).

Local Government, Municipality, and Disaster Response

MacManus et al. (2006) argue that the major responsibility of responding to disasters falls under the jurisdiction of local government. While Elsworth et al. (2007) argued that local governments accept this role, there are many barriers that prevent them from properly adopting this responsibility. These barriers include the lack of financial resources such as funding as well as human resources in the form of emergency management staff. These barriers also include gaps in risk assessment and information as well as lack of communication with other agencies. Furthermore, community preparedness and education about disaster management are usually lacking.

Kusumasari et al. (2010) presented a comprehensive literature review about the capabilities of local governments in disaster management. They argued that the capabilities of local government are affected by budget, staff, and expertise. Constraints often do exist because of the lack of coordination and community engagement. Recently, studies emerged about local governments' roles in disaster management. These roles revolve around the following (Kusumasari et al., 2010): (1) disaster management should be implemented by local governments (Perry & Mushkatel, 1984), (2) local governments are the major players and the most active in disaster response (Herman, 1982; Labadie, 1984), (3) a recent trend of shifting and decentralizing disaster management from the central to local governments (May, 1985), (4) the importance of adopting a community-based approach to disaster response (Cigler, 1987).

Solwan (2004), as quoted by Kusumasari et al. (2010, p. 442), summarized the main tasks of local governments when managing disasters:

- Identifying vulnerable people and areas within the district.
- Ensuring that all members of the community are aware of the potential effects of natural disasters.
- Disseminating advice notes and good practice guides for disaster mitigation to the community.
- Maintaining contact with officials responsible for planning, construction, health, and welfare, by issuing warnings, or providing fire, and crowd control systems.
- Ensuring that members of the community receive suitable first aid training.
- Implementing community education and awareness programs by working with educational institutions.
- Assisting and helping refugees.

Local Government's Response to Disaster in Developing Countries

Local governments in developing countries lack responsiveness to disasters (Kusumasari et al., 2010). Indeed, in developing contexts, plans for coordination are usually absent between stakeholders at the local government; and in many cases local government must consult with and follow the guidelines of the central government on the proper way to respond (Hoetmer, 1983; Perry & Mushkatel, 1984; Wolensky & Wolensky, 1990; Kusumasari et al., 2010). Moreover, literature argues that local governments in developing contexts usually allocate low priorities and budgets to developing a comprehensive disaster management plan (Cigler, 1987). Another reason for failure to respond to disaster was that most officials consider disaster planning as a product rather than a process. Hence, these officials tend to isolate disaster planning from the daily planning process, and they assign this task to organizations that are separated from institutionalized sources of social power in the community (Wenger et al., 1980; Kusumasari et al., 2010). Another reason for the failure of local governments in disaster response is the lack of proper planning and implementation, blurry lines of authorities, lack of proper channels of dissemination of information, absence of interorganizational coordination, and abuse of established planning procedures (Dynes et al., 1972; Turner, 1976a).

These problems in developing countries occur because of many issues: (1) stakeholders view disasters as Acts of God and unexpected events, and thus do not take them seriously as they do not want to incur high costs in preparing for them (Kusumasari et al., 2010); (2) the presence of ineffective leadership in addition to political pressures play a crucial role in lack of planning (Rossi et al., 1982). Labadie (1984b) also summarized the issues faced in local management of emergencies. Usually, emergency managers in local governments are placed under a line agency and compete for limited funding. Furthermore, due to the rigid bureaucratic systems reallocation of budgets for response become difficult. As such, when disaster strikes, communication and coordination between the departments become difficult.

Military Role

Military forces play crucial roles in responding to natural disasters in affected states (Harvey, 2009). The decision-making process skills, in addition to logistical and coordination capacities of the army, allow them to contribute to an effective humanitarian response during disasters (Wilder, 2008); this point is in light when many humanitarian actors are willing to collaborate with the national army when disaster strikes (Harvey, 2009). However, the literature does not cover the role of military forces in responding to disaster

(Harvey, 2009). Most of the guidelines and literature on the use of military assets usually focus on the role of international forces (UN, 2003; UN, 2006) and do not focus on the relationship between humanitarian actors and the military forces of the affected states (Harvey, 2009).

Trust in the military as a responder in post-disaster situations has been a controversial topic (Malesic, 2015). While some argue that this would lead to a militarization of the disaster response, others argue that military assistance is significant mainly because this stakeholder has the required skillset and resources to assist in the response. On the other hand, members of the military consider this response as a window to improve public image and legitimacy. Malesic (2015) further argues that in disaster response, the civilian disaster management structures usually compete with the military structure and become reluctant to ask for military help in the early stages as they fear that their culture and values would be affected when they cooperate with the military.

Community and Disaster Response

The fourth strand of literature on disaster management focuses on the role of communities, social capital, and associations. Although a large body of empirical literature addresses emergency preparedness and what happens during a disaster, there is limited focus on post-disaster issues such as how communities contribute to direct response. In addition, there is limited research that considers both the networks of physical infrastructure and social ties present in a community to address issues related to post-disaster recovery. Most studies have treated resilience as a technocratic rather than a social problem by examining the scope and speed of rebuilding as functions of the level of damage and the amount of aid (Dacy & Kunreuther, 1969; Kamel & Loukaitou-Sideris, 2004; Sadri et al., 2018). Moreover, literature on disaster management focuses on the crucial role of volunteers and nonprofit associations in adapting to change during the recovery phase (Paterson et al., 2020).

Research on democracy and political participation in earlier scholarly work views the importance of community, religion, family, social organizations, namely: civil society (Skocpol et al., 2000; Skocpol & Fiorina, 1999; Greeley, 1997; Verba et al., 1995; Weil, 1994; Weil, 1989; Lipset, 1981; Verba & Nie, 1972; Patterson & Weil, 2010). In this regard, Tocqueville argued that due to their nature, community organizations are more responsive than central governments since they are more rapid, consistent, and flexible due to their interest in the common good (Patterson & Weil, 2010). Based on Tocqueville, citizens can act as a community through civil society associations and can respond to issues by joining their efforts toward a common cause and common good. In Tocqueville's argument, community organizations are better and more effective than the central government since they are flexible, adaptive, and consistent. Local communities have the knowledge and the common good as a priority as opposed to the central government that is more atomized (Patterson & Weil, 2010). In this regard, there is a need to consider local community and nonstate actors when discussing disaster management.

Literature on analyzing disaster argues that preparedness and recovery stresses on the importance of the intangible social phenomena of resilience and its role in effective response to disaster (Patterson & Weil, 2010). This social resilience is strongly present in social theories and focuses on the role of "social capital", mainly social networks that help individuals reach better results than if they were working through isolated efforts (Sampson et al., 2005; Putnam & Feldstein, 2003; Lin et al., 2001; Putnam, 2000; Coleman, 1990). Putnam defined social capital as the extent to which individuals are involved in informal networks or formal civic organizations (Putnam, 1995, 2001). Social capital has been intensively researched (Putnam, Leonardi, and Nanetti, 1993; Bourdieu, 1986; Coleman, 1990) and acknowledges both the self-interest of actors and the influence of the social and economic context (Karner, 2001). In fact, Putnam stressed the importance of the relationship between the different actors within the society, arguing that features of social organization, such as trust, norms, and networks, can improve the efficiency of society by facilitating coordinated actions (Putnam et al., 1993). Dynes (2006) argued that the key to a successful response to disasters involves access to social capital. Other scholars, such as Wachtendorf and Kendra (2004), also concluded that social capital and expertise are crucial in disaster recovery, since social capital, as opposed to conventional measures, provides an explanation of the recovery of some areas faster than others and how neighborhoods that already have existing activities are faster in recovery (Aldrich, 2012).

Role of Volunteers

The inclusion of volunteers in disaster response is crucial for proper response. When disasters strike, unorganized individuals are usually the actual first responders (Neal & Phillips, 1995; Drabek & McEntire, 2003; Johansson et al., 2018). These players often present a significant contribution in disaster response and are viewed as "filling the void" when an emergency response organization fails to do so (Neal & Phillips, 1995; Drabek & McEntire, 2003; Johansson et al., 2018). These same volunteers are sometimes viewed as causing trouble mainly because they do not have the required skills for intervention and are viewed by professional emergency responders as a mixed blessing (Johansson et al., 2018; Barsky, Trainor,

Torres, & Aguirre, 2007; Harris, Shaw, Scully, Smith, & Hieke, 2017). Indeed, unaffiliated volunteers are not involved in disaster response activities and usually lack the relevant organizational affiliation.

In addition to these unaffiliated volunteers, there are other types of voluntary actors on the ground (Johansson et al., 2018). These could include voluntary organizations or professional organizations that act on a voluntary basis (Moynihan, 2009). Three types of voluntary actors appear during disaster response: (1) organized volunteers, (2) participants in emergent groups, and (3) individual unaffiliated volunteers (Johansson et al., 2018). Most of the literature on volunteers in disaster response focuses on individual informal volunteers (Barsky et al., 2007; Harris et al., 2017; Helsloot & Ruitenberg, 2004; Kvarnlof & Johansson, 2014; Scanlon et al., 2014). Once these individual volunteers start to converge, they organize their activities and create emergent groups (Johansson, 2018), and are viewed as a group of people who were in the same emergency place and who engage in the same action (Johansson, 2018). Stallings and Quarantelli (185:84) defined emergent groups as "private citizens who work together in pursuit of collective goals relevant to actual or potential disasters but whose organization has not yet become institutionalized". In addition, Johansson et al., 2018, p. 520) defined emergent as "the newness, absence of formalization and lack of tradition that characterize this kind of group". Moreover, the available literature studied the role of voluntary organizations during disaster response (Lundberg, Tornqvist, & Nadjm-Tehrani, 2014) and focused mostly on developed contexts, arguing that to succeed, voluntary organizations should be well-established and legitimate (Luna, 2002). Only then will a collaboration between the latter and professional response organization succeed (Johansson, 2018).

Role of Local Associations in Disaster Response

Local-based organizations are grassroots organizations that have many characteristics. In disaster management, these organizations have a crucial role in creating and distributing social capital (Aldrich & Meyer, 2015; Eikenberry, Arroyave, & Cooper, 2007). As opposed to the government, these associations can directly respond to the need of the society without the need to go through the administrative bureaucratic cycle, as they can directly identify and respond to the crisis (Byron, 2010; IFRC, 2015).

Many pieces of literature were presented to illustrate the importance and readiness of these organizations in disaster management and in the allocation of resources for building resilience (Storr & Haeffele-Balch, 2012; Bolin & Stanford, 1998; Rivera & Nickels, 2014), especially as these organizations should be more involved in the community. Blackman et al. (2017,

p. 95) observe that "a lack of community involvement and agency may largely explain the lack of effective long-term disaster recovery". However, one issue that might affect these organizations' success is the limited capacity in financial and human resources. In addition, most of these organizations are not involved or have limited involvement in disaster management structures in the governmental plans (Kapucu, 2006; Comfort & Kapucu, 2006). Failure to engage local organizations in planning would in turn lead to uncoordinated activities, duplication of work, and the failure to provide an effective response to disaster, while large organizations such as the Red Cross are usually incorporated in the disaster response system (Eller, Gerber, & Robinson, 2018). Unfortunately, smaller organizations that usually leverage social capital are not included (Hutton, 2018; Paterson et al., 2010). Another type of volunteering during disaster extends to private for-profit organizations that usually do not conduct voluntary work but exceptionally place their knowledge and skills to assist in the response activity (Kendra et al., 2003; Majchrzak et al., 2007). Voluntary emergency for-profit organizations have an emergency response at their core activities to assist professional responders during an emergency (Johansson, 2018).

Disaster Response in Developing Context

The state should be the major player in disaster response; every aspect of coordination and collaboration should be initiated at the level of the national government; however, this is not the case in the context of developing countries. On paper, every country acknowledges its responsibilities toward its citizens in times of crisis; however, this is not always the case (Walker et al., 2008). Throughout history, many governments were successful in their disaster risk reduction (DRR) policies, while others were not. This failure in DRR is mainly viewed in the literature as a result of weak governments, and the lack of political will (Jones et al., 2015; William, 2011).

When researching the literature on disaster and fragile or weak states, it is important to discuss the definition of a fragile state. The main characteristics are the lack of capacity and capability in addition to willingness and legitimacy to perform its main functions (Harvey, 2009). Chandran and Jones (2008) analyzed state capacity and concluded that there are three different types or categories of states.

- A clear and emerging social contract that exists between the state and its citizens.
  - The main role of the state is to assist and protect its citizens when disasters strike. In such cases, international humanitarian actors are willing to support and build capacity for an effective response.

- Weak states with limited resources and capabilities.
  - These states are unable to face responsibilities and assist the citizens during disasters. When these states are unable but willing to assist in the disasters, international humanitarian actors might assist through substitution and capacity building.
- States that do not have the capability and will to negotiate a social contract.
  - These do not assist nor protect their citizens in time of disaster. In such cases, international actors might present both substitution and advocacy to encourage these states to fulfill their duties.

Conclusion

Since good governance is crucial in disaster response, this chapter reviewed the different literature and conceptual framework addressing state–nonprofit relationship and argued that the major factors determining this relationship are autonomy, partnership, and solidarity. Moreover, it reviewed this relationship in disaster response and argued that based on the literature, three characteristics are required in disaster recovery: (1) interorganizational structures, (2) trust in the relationship, and (3) role clarity. Since trust is a major player in disaster response, the second section expanded on the importance of building mutual trust between the different players as a way of reaching success in disaster response and recovery. To come up with a successful disaster response strategy, there is a need to build trust between different players in disaster management, namely, public institutions and the government, disaster survivors and nonstate actors; hence, it is crucial to have trust in authority and the institutions, as well as establish a credible social context. It further reviewed the complex relationship that appears during disaster response and the importance of cooperation and coordination. Disasters can overwhelm the resources of governments that are then often reliant on support from the nonprofit sector. Due to the increased reliance on support from nonprofit sector organizations in disasters, there is a raised interest in evaluating how organizations from the nonprofit and public sectors engage in interorganizational collaboration during disasters and how those involved can overcome barriers to collaboration.

This chapter has reviewed the role of local players in disaster response and analyzed the role played by the national government, local government, and the army in both developed and developing contexts. Moreover, it reviewed the role of nonstate actors, mainly local communities, volunteers, and nonprofit organizations. In this regard, it argued that irrespective of the structure of the disaster management units, the literature distinguishes four major responsibilities of the state: (1) declaring the state of emergency, (2) assisting and protecting the population, (3) monitoring and coordinating assistance, and (4) ensuring the functioning of an adequate normative framework. Moreover, the level of development of the state directly affects the success of the disaster response. There are four general categories of determinants: (1) economic factors, (2) political structure and environment, (3) social factors, and (4) historical factors. Recent studies have argued that corruption in the public sector and natural disaster are related. Indeed, corrupt states are affected the most in times of natural disaster, especially in the number of deaths and the level of destruction, as compared to less corrupt countries.

Since the responsibility of disaster response falls directly under the jurisdiction of local governments and municipalities, this chapter further reviewed the role of the latter in developed and developing contexts. It also reviewed the crucial role played by military forces. Local-based organizations are grassroots organizations that have many characteristics. In disaster management, these organizations have a crucial role in creating and distributing social capital. As opposed to the government, these associations can directly respond to the needs of the society without the need to go through the administrative bureaucratic cycle, as they can directly identify and respond to the crisis.

References

Almond, G. A., & Verba, S. (1965). *The civic culture: Political attitudes and democracy in five nations. An analytic study.* Boston, MA, and Toronto, ON: Little, Brown and Company.

Barsky, L. E., Trainor, J. E., Torres, M. R., & Aguirre, B. E. (2007). Managing volunteers: FEMA's urban search and rescue program and interactions with unaffiliated responders in disaster response. *Disasters, 31*(4), 495–507. https://doi.org/10.1111/j.1467-7717.2007.01021.x.

Calossi, E., Sberna, S., & Vannucci, A. (2012). Disasters and corruption, corruption as disaster. In *International disaster response law* (pp. 651–683). T. M. C. Asser Press. https://doi.org/10.1007/978-90-6704-882-8_27.

Chandran, R., & Jones, B. (2008). Concepts and dilemmas of state building in fragile situations: From fragility to resilience. *Journal on Development, 9*(3).

Cigler, B. A. (1987). Emergency management and public administration. In M. T. Charles & J. C. K. Kim (Eds.), *Crisis management* (pp. 5–19). Springfield, MO: A Case Book, Thomas.

Cvetkovich, G., & Löfstedt, R. E. (Eds.). (1999). *Social trust and the management of risk.* London: Earthscan.

Drabek, T. E., & McEntire, D. A. (2003). Emergent phenomena and the sociology of disaster: Lessons, trends, and opportunities from the research literature. *Disaster Prevention and management: An International Journal, 12*(2), 97–112. https://doi.org/10.1108/09653560310474214.

Dynes, R. R., Quarantelli, E. L., & Kreps, G. A. (1972). *A perspective on disaster planning*. Columbus, OH: Disaster Research Center, Ohio State University.

Elsworth, G., & Anthony-Harvey-Beavis, K. (2007). *The national local government emergency management survey* - Final Report, (C. a. L. i. E. The Collaboration for Interdisciplinary Research, Trans.). In RMIT University Circle (Ed.), (pp. 54). Melbourne, Victoria, Australia: RMIT University.

Escaleras, M., Anbarci, N., & Register, C. A. (2007). Public sector corruption and major earthquakes: A potentially deadly interaction. *Public Choice, 132*(1/2), 209–230. https://doi.org/10.1007/s11127-007-9148-y.

Escaleras, M., & Register, C. (2016). Public sector corruption and natural hazards. *Public Finance Review, 44*(6), 746–768. https://doi.org/10.1177/1091142115613155.

Green, P. (2005). Disaster by design: Corruption, construction and catastrophe. *The British Journal of Criminology, 45*(4), 528–546. http://www.jstor.org/stable/23639253.

Hardin, R. (1999). Do we want trust in government? In M. E. Warren (Ed.), *Democracy and trust* (pp. 22–42). Cambridge: Cambridge University Press.

Harris, M., Shaw, D., Scully, J., Smith, C. M., & Hieke, G. (2017). The involvement/exclusion paradox of spontaneous volunteering: New lessons and theory from winter flood episodes in England. *Nonprofit and Voluntary Sector Quarterly, 46*(2), 352–371. https://doi.org/10.1177/0899764016654222.

Harvey, P. (2009). *Towards good government: The role of the affected state in disaster response*. Humanitarian Policy Group, ODI. London, United Kingdom.

Helsloot, I., & Ruitenberg, A. (2004). Citizen response to disaster: A survey of literature and some practical implications. *Journal of Contingencies and Crisis Management, 12*(3), 98–111. https://doi.org/10.1111/j.0966-0879.2004.00440.x.

Herman, R. E. (1982). *Disaster planning for local government*. New York: Universe.

Hoetmer, G. J. (1983). *Emergency management individual and county data*. Baseline Data Reports 15. Washington, DC: International City Management Association.

IFRC. (2007). *Annotations to the draft guidelines for the domestic facilitation and regulation of international disaster relief and initial recovery assistance*. International Federation of the Red Cross and Red Crescent Societies. Geneva.

Inglehart, R. (1990). *Culture shift in advanced industrial society*. Princeton, NJ: Princeton University Press.

Johansson, R., Danielsson, E., Kvarnlof, L., Eriksson, K., & Karlsson, R. (2018). At the external boundary of a disaster response operation: The dynamics of volunteer inclusion. *Contingencies and Crisis Management, 26*(4), 519–529.

Kang, S., & Skidmore, M. (2018). The effects of natural disasters on social trust: Evidence from South Korea. *Sustainability, 10*(9), 1–16.

Kendra, J. M., Wachtendorf, T., & Quarantelli, E. L. (2003). The evacuation of lower Manhattan by water transport on September 11: An unplanned success. *Joint Commission Journal on Quality and Patient Safety, 30*(5), 316–318. https://doi.org/10.1016/S1549-3741(03)29036-5.

Kervyn, N., Chan, E., Malone, C., Korpusik, A., & Ybarra, O. (2014). Not all disasters are equal in the public's eye: The negativity effect of warmth and brand perception. *Social Cognition, 32*(3), 256–275.

Kratcoski, P. C. (2018). *Fraud and corruption in times of disaster. Fraud and corruption* (pp. 139–157). Springer International Publishing. https://doi.org/10.1007/978-3-319-92333-8_8.

Kusumasari, B., Alam, Q., & Siddiqui, K. (2010). Resource capability for local government in managing disaster. *Disaster Prevention and Management, 19*(4), 438–451.

Kvarnlof, L., & Johansson, R. (2014). Boundary practices at incident sites: Making distinctions between emergency personnel and the public. *International Journal of Emergency Services, 3*(1), 65–76. https://doi.org/10.1108/IJES-01-2013-0002.

Labadie, J. R. (1984a). Defining the role of an emergency manager. *Small Town, 14,* 19–21.

Labadie, J. R. (1984b). Problems in local emergency management. *Environmental Management, 8*(6), 489–494.

Liang, Y. (2016). Trust in Chinese government and Quality of Life (QOL) of Sichuan Earthquake Survivors: Does trust in government help to promote QOL? *Social Indicators Research, 127*(2), 541–564.

Löfstedt, R. E. (2005). *Risk management in post-trust societies.* Houndmills and New York: Palgrave Macmillan.

Lundberg, J., Tornqvist, E. K., & Nadjm-Tehrani, S. (2014). Establishing conversation spaces in hastily formed networks: The worst fire in modern Swedish history. *Disasters, 38*(4), 790–807. https://doi.org/10.1111/disa.12076.

MacManus, S. A., & Caruson, K. (2006). Code Red: Florida City and county officials rate threat information sources and the homeland security advisory system. *State and Local Government Review, 38*(1), 12–22.

Majchrzak, A., Jarvenpaa, S. L., & Hollingshead, A. B. (2007). Coordinating expertise among emergent groups responding to disasters. *Organization Science, 18*(1), 147–161. https://doi.org/10.1287/orsc.1060.0228.

Malešič, M. (2015). The impact of military engagement in disaster management on civil-military relations. *Current Sociology, 63*(7), 980–998.

Malesic, M. (2019). The concept of trust in disasters: The Slovenian experience. *Disaster Prevention and Management, 28*(5), 603–615.

Maxwell, D., & Walker, P. (2008). *Shaping the humanitarian world.* London: Taylor, and Francis Ltd.

May, P. J. (1985). *Recovering from catastrophes: Federal disaster relief policy and politics.* Westport, CT: Greenwood.

Mishler, W., & Rose, R. (2001). What are the origins of political trust? Testing institutional and cultural theories in post-communist societies. *Comparative Political Studies, 34*(1), 30–62.

Moynihan, D. P. (2009). The network governance of crisis response: Case studies of incident command systems. *Journal of Public Administration Research and Theory, 19*(4), 895–915. https://doi.org/10.1093/jopart/mun033.

Neal, D. M., & Phillips, B. D. (1995). Effective emergency management: Reconsidering the bureaucratic approach. *Disasters, 19*(4), 327–337. https://doi.org/10.1111/j.1467-7717.1995.tb00353.x.

Nikolova, E., & Marinov, N. (2017). Do public fund windfalls increase corruption? Evidence from a natural disaster. *Comparative Political Studies, 50*(11), 1455–1488. https://doi.org/10.1177/0010414016679109.

O'Callaghan, S., & Pantualiano, S. (2007). *Protective action: Incorporating civilian protection into humanitarian response*, HPG Report 26. London: Overseas Development Institute.

Perry, R. W., & Mushkatel, A. H. (1984). *Disaster management: Warning response and community relocations.* Westport, CT: Quorum.

Putnam, R. D. (2001). *Bowling alone.* New York: The Collapse and Revival of American Community, Simon and Schuster.

Rossi, P. H., Wright, J. D., & Weber-Burdin, E. (1982). *Natural hazards and public choice: The state and local politics of hazard mitigation.* New York: Academic.

Scanlon, J., Helsloot, I., & Groenendaal, J. (2014). Putting it all together: Integrating ordinary people into emergency response. *International Journal of Mass Emergencies and Disasters, 32*(1), 43–63.

Schupp, R., Loveridge, S., Skidmore, M., Lim, J., & Rogers, C. (2017). Trust and patience after Tornado. *Weather, Climate and Society, 9*(4), 659–668.

Shughart, I. I., & W. F. (2011). Disaster relief as bad public policy. *Independent Review (Oakland, Calif.), 15*(4), 519–539.

Thoresen, S., Birkeland, M. S., Wenzel-Larsen, T., & Blix, I. (2018). Loss of trust may never heal. Institutional trust in disaster victims in a long-term perspective: Associations with social support and mental health. *Frontiers in Psychology, 9*(July), 1–10.

Turner, B. A. (1976). The development of disaster – A sequence model for the analysis of the origins of disasters. *Sociological Review, 24*(4), 753–774.

Warren, M. E. (1999). Democratic theory and trust. In M. E. Warren (Ed.), *Democracy and trust* (pp. 310–345). Cambridge: Cambridge University Press.

Wenger, D. E., James, T. F., & Faupel, C. F. (1980). *Disaster beliefs and emergency planning. Disaster research project.* Newark, DE: University of Delaware.

White, J. D., & Fu, K. W. (2012). Who do you trust? Comparing people-centered communications in disaster situations in the United States and China. *Journal of Comparative Policy Analysis, 14*(2), 126–142.

Wolensky, R. P., & Wolensky, K. C. (1990). Local government's problem with disaster management: A literature review and structural analysis. *Policy Studies Review, 9*(4), 703–725.

Yamamura, E. (2014). Impact of natural disaster on public sector corruption. *Public Choice, 161*(3/4), 385–405. https://doi.org/10.1007/s11127-014-0154-6.

3 Setting the Scene of Disaster Management in Lebanon

Public Administration, Corruption, and the Role of Local and International Organizations in Lebanon

Introduction

Lebanon is governed by a consociational democracy. This type of democracy emerged after the independence of the state from the French mandate in 1943. While this consociational democracy allowed the state to access an increased level of freedom and civil rights as compared to other Arab countries, this same system did not protect the state from social and religious division, nor from destabilizing and negative regional and international influences. Indeed, this system was not strong enough and shifted due to internal and external dynamics and was tested on many occasions. Moreover, Lebanon does not possess governmental mechanisms of accountability to regulate politicians' actions. Lebanon was ranked 149 out of 180 on Transparency International's Corruption Perceptions Index in 2020 (Transparency International, 2020). This number indicates that Lebanon is a highly corrupt state. Indeed, this corruption resulted in the Lebanese distrust in public institutions, the absence of anti-corruption mechanisms, and the lack of understanding of the causes and consequences of corruption (Lebanese Transparency Association, 2009).

This political system and the high level of corruption affected disaster management policies in Lebanon. Many instances reveal that the Lebanese government has either failed to respond to disasters or removed itself from the response and recovery phase, leaving space for different actors to support the society. While the High Relief Commission, The Lebanese Army, and the National Council for the Environment are the main governmental bodies responsible for disaster management, other bodies also work on relief, mainly local governments, and municipality unions are the ones directly responding to disasters. In different instances throughout history, nonprofit organizations have stepped in to replace the role of the weak state. During disasters, the relationship of these organizations with the government was

DOI: 10.4324/9781003222545-4

either cooperative or noncooperative, where the latter totally withdrew from the field.

The main aim of this chapter is to set the political and administrative scene leading to the Beirut August 4 explosion through reviewing the literature on Lebanese public administration, corruption, economic policies, disaster management policies, and the historical role of organizations in responding to disasters in Lebanon.

In this regard, this chapter will review the effect of the state's sociopolitical infrastructure on disaster management and mainly respond by looking at (1) public administration and corruption and poverty in Lebanon, (2) disaster management policy in the state of Lebanon, and (3) the role of local and international nonprofit associations.

Public Administration and Corruption in Lebanon

Public administration in the Middle East is faced with many challenges (Ahmad Al-Qarioti & Al-Enezi, 2004; El-Zein & Sims, 2004; Hatem, 1994; Iles, Almhedie, & Baruch, 2012; Jreisat, 1970, 1989; Kisirwani, 1997; Nakib & Palmer, 1976). Moreover, literature on public administration in the region has focused on the difficulties in developing the administrative functions (Bachir, 1997; Crow & Iskandar, 1961; Hassan & Sarker, 2012; Jreisat, 1990, 1999, 2006). These challenges vary from underperforming and unproductive employees to rigid bureaucracies to lack of administrative innovations (Jreisat, 2006).

In Lebanon, public administration is intertwined with sectarian politics, especially since sectarian politics is at the heart of the administration of the state (Haase et al., 2018). In fact, the Lebanese political structure was based on the National Pact of 1943, which reinforced sectarianism in public institutions and turned the state into an establishment that is highly sectarian, focused on representing religious and ethnic groups (Kisirwani & Parle, 1987). The National Pact of 1943, a verbal agreement between two political leaders from two different religious communities Bechara El Khoury, a Christian Maronite, and Riad el Soleh, a Muslim Sunni, was the beginning of consociationalism in Lebanon. It is based on the proportionality principle between religions by first fixing the ratio of Christian to Muslim in the parliament and then by dividing the top three positions between the Christian Maronite, Muslim Sunni, and Muslim Shia (Bagaards, 2019). The National Pact opened the door for nepotism, corruption, and patronage. Institutions in Lebanon were in turn restrained by "centralization of the power, outdated bureaucratic structures and administrative knowledge" (Haase, 2018).

Public administration in Lebanon was also wrecked by the Civil War. Indeed, this war destroyed the infrastructure of the state, transforming its institutions into a shelter for militias and political parties (Adwan, 2004; El-Zein & Holly Sims, 2004; Mehanna, 1993). The Lebanese Civil War further entrenched sectarianism into the political and social life in Lebanon by removing any sense of national unity and social cohesion (Haase, 2018), and unfortunately this system of sectarianism continued after the war (Ghosn & Khoury, 2011). The Lebanese Civil War emphasized the inherent deficiencies in the state of Lebanon (Jawad, 2009). Furthermore, the sectarian structure and the lack of internal cohesiveness, together with external political interference from foreign powers, sped up the collapse of the state. With the end of the Civil War, the state emerged as a weak entity and began contracting social services to private and volunteer organizations. It is indeed the weakness and the failure of the state and the absence of any legitimate power to control this sector that allowed these organizations and groups to develop and thrive.

In postwar Lebanon, the government initiated programs for reforms such as introducing public budgeting and financial processes (Haase, 2018) and establishing the Office of the Minister of State for Administrative Reform (OMSAR), which was responsible for overseeing the development of the bureaucracy; however, all these efforts were hindered by many obstacles (OMSAR, 2011).

Indeed, Lebanese administration is facing many problems in governance (AbouAssi et al., 2013; Kisirwani & Parle, 1987; OMSAR, 2011). First, the system is based on nepotism, patronage, and corruption (Atzili, 2010; el-Saad, 2001; El-Zein & Holly Sims, 2004; Haase, 2018), and the centralized bureaucracy is unresponsive to the needs of citizens, mainly ones from lower socioeconomic communities (AbouAssi et al., 2013; el-Saad, 2001).

The capacity of the Lebanese bureaucracies and agencies is always highlighted and tested (Haase et al., 2018). The OMSAR discussed the problems facing this bureaucracy (2011). The report argued that the bureaucracy is threatened by the deficiencies in the planning and policymaking in the country, in addition to a highly centralized government, obsolete administrative structures, lack of e-governance, and the political unwillingness to reform the administration (OMSAR, 2011; Haase et al., 2018). The report also discussed the role of individual public administrators in Lebanon and the lack of knowledge they have mainly in strategic management; program management; decision-making, public budgeting, and ethics. The report stressed the importance of restructuring the public institutions in Lebanon and called on the urgency of establishing a competent system of public administration that recruits qualified staff (OMSAR, 2011) in addition to recruiting adequate staff with leadership skills. The report further discussed the shortage of staff, which is also linked to the lack of competencies of the public officials who are incapable of responding to the administrative needs of the country (OMSAR, 2011). The report further highlighted that although there is a great need of public administrators in the country, this is not a priority in higher education.

Moreover, in a study conducted on the content of advertised public administration courses in higher education institutions in Lebanon, Haase et al. (2018) argued that the major topics needed for proper functioning of the Lebanese administration are missing, such as budgeting and financial processes, decision-making, citizen engagement, and human resources. These are the same challenges faced in the Lebanese administrative system (Haase et al., 2018). Moreover, the study revealed that public administration students are not getting the soft skills training needed to succeed as public officials.

While many international initiatives were presented to help the government on the issue of transparency, management techniques, and focus on information technology in service delivery, most of these initiatives were constrained by the political system in the state (Bhuiyan et al., 2020), labeled by many as being dysfunctional (Makdisi, Kiwan, & Marktanner, 2011; Salamey, 2014; Haase, 2018), especially that it does not allow individual citizens to participate in the decision-making process and allows political parties to establish clientelist relationships that supersede people's demands (Makdisi et al., 2011; Safa, 2010; Haase, 2018).

Throughout Lebanon's history, anti-corruption laws were obstructed by the absence of political will to combat corruption. Indeed, enacting any law in Lebanon is subject to a long slow process. Thus, the anti-corruption law took more than ten years to be enacted: for example, drafted in June 2008, the "Financial Disclosure and the Punishment of Illicit Enrichment Law" (Law No. 189/2020) was enacted in 2020, after 12 years. Another example is law no 175/2020, adopted after 11 years of its proposal. This latter covers the anti-corruption law in the public sector and calls for the creation of a National Commission to Combat Corruption (NACC) (Al Moghabat, 2020). The NACC is the main entity responsible for implementation of all anti-corruption laws.

This slow process is the consequence of the lack of will of politicians to pass laws that might harm their sects and political parties. Since corruption in Lebanon is embedded in public institutions and Lebanese citizens, working on anti-corruption law faces several limitations.

Even though Lebanon moved closer to combatting corruption, these laws remain not fully implemented.

Due to these reasons, Lebanon has been unable to address all its socioeconomic problems. To this day, most of the country does not receive more than four hours of electricity per day, there is an absence of clean water, poor sanitation, deficient urban planning, and lack of proper and basic transportation infrastructure (Haase, 2018). All the above problems have resulted in a weak state that is unable to provide basic needs to its citizens. Poverty is a serious social problem in Lebanon despite some apparent improvements in the last decade. The harsh economic situation that the Lebanese experience is mostly a result of economic policies that the state has followed since the end of the Civil War. Indeed, the state does not provide the minimum social rights for its citizens, and as such allows sectarian parties to provide services for their own communities for political aims. ESCWA estimated that in 2020 around 55 percent of the Lebanese population, or an estimate of 2.7 million Lebanese, lived below the poverty line, while 23 percent lived in extreme poverty. Poverty is distributed in different regions in the country: the highest poverty rate is witnessed in the three areas of Hermel, Baalbeck, and Akkar. The largest cities in the country – Beirut, Saida, and Tripoli – have witnessed an increase in poverty rates, mainly perceived through child labor and overcrowding. In addition, the unemployment rate in Lebanon is the highest among the poorest populations, most of whom consist of unskilled workers.

Disaster Management in Lebanon

It is estimated that more than three million people in Lebanon are facing food and water insecurity and diseases. This insecurity has recently increased due to the high number of Syrian refugee influx, the current economic crisis in Lebanon, and the effect of COVID-19, in addition to the nature of the geographic regions in Lebanon that are exposed to flooding, droughts, forest fires, and earthquakes (Murched et al., 2015). It is important to note that Lebanon is a signatory of the Hyogo Framework for Action, which promotes the reduction of disaster risk, and which commits the state to work on developmental planning to protect the environment and present social and economic developmental plans to develop the infrastructure and work with vulnerable populations on disaster preparedness through education, food security, and health care strategies. Although Lebanon has ratified Hyogo Framework for Action in 2001, the government has stated that it failed to meet the framework's aspiration, blaming the issue on budgetary support and political instability (Fawaz, 2020).

Since its independence, the Lebanese state has been subject to many disasters, whether they are man-made or natural. Recently, the Syrian refugee crisis, in addition to the devaluation of the Lebanese pound, has undermined the capacity of the central, local, and municipal levels.

Natural disasters have included threats of severe earthquakes, floods, forest fires, and droughts (Murshed, 2015). Those disasters were coupled with a highly centralized state, unregulated urban expansion, land use (Murshed, 2015), irregular human and industrial waste, and construction without government supervision, in addition to an absence of national disaster management plan. In all these cases, the government either failed to respond to these events or withdrew from the recovery phase, leaving space for different actors to support the society. The Syrian refugee crisis has directly affected the capacity of local authorities in Lebanon. The authorities were already suffering from lack of capacity to provide public services for their constituents. Moreover, these local governments lack the capacity to build clear disaster risk reduction plans, let alone clear preparedness and response; the absence of clear codes for land and urban planning codes also affected the disaster risk reduction plans in the state (Murched et al., 2015).

As highlighted in the examples below, all these disasters have had social, political, and economic consequences and have highlighted the weakness of the state. In 2005, the government deployed 10,000 personnel to manage a snowstorm; in 2006, the government delivered relief assistance to the displaced (Shearer & Pickup, 2007; Haase, 2014); in 2008, an Ethiopian airline crashed into the Mediterranean; in 2012, a building collapsed, killing 27 and injuring 11; and in 2019, a fire forest destroyed around 2000 ha of green lands in Mechref area. In each of these events, power sharing, in addition to the lack of coordination, showed the failure of the government (Haase, 2014) as the Lebanese government failed to initiate a disaster management strategy, due to the political and administrative deadlock that has been present since the end of the war (Haase, 2014). Corrupt construction practices have led to disasters and a high number of deaths (Saharan, 2015). In 1999, it was revealed that the collapse of buildings was mostly the result of corrupt construction practices (Saharan, 2015).

Indeed, Lebanon lacks a clear disaster risk management system, including a lack of effective policies, functioning institutions, early warning systems, and technical know-how, in addition to awareness at the societal level besides preparedness. While many strategies were presented by international organizations to assist Lebanon in placing a clear strategy for disaster risk reduction, most of these plans were faced with deadlocks created by the dynamics of the political system (Murched et al., 2015). The complex political system in Lebanon has directly affected the developmental challenges and risks faced in Lebanon as decision-making is always delayed and any policy would lead to political and social tensions (Murched et al., 2015). Lebanon is facing many risks from natural hazards, ranging from earthquakes and tsunamis to floods, forest fires, and drought. This is also increased by the lack of presence of the government ministries in the peripheries in addition to the lack of clear urban planning expansion and enforcement of building codes and environmental factors such as poor sanitation and environmental pollution (Murched et al., 2015). Moreover, the political instability in the region is also directly affecting the state of Lebanon as it might face influxes of internally displaced peoples, such as when this happened in the 2006 war, or the Syrian refugee crisis resulting in more than 1.6 million Syrian refugees. Any earthquake would lead to a huge disaster in Lebanon and would cause major fatalities due to the absence of an effective disaster risk reduction strategy. Although Lebanon has witnessed many earthquakes in addition to recurring floods and deforestation, no early warning system or community preparedness has been adopted by the central or the local governments. While many initiates were created to respond to forest fires, there is a lack of community preparedness and awareness (Murched et al., 2015).

Indeed, risk hazards in Lebanon were caused by many factors, including environmental degradation, unplanned urban expansion, lack of solid waste management, habitation near riverbeds, and poor land use management. Thus, the vulnerability of the society to disaster risks has increased over the years, especially with the lack of preventive actions by both the Lebanese government and the society (Murched et al., 2015). When it comes to disaster management in Lebanon, most of the efforts are always directed to relief post-disaster rather than prevention and reduction.

Moreover, lack of coordination between the different agencies responsible for disaster management, in addition to lack of awareness of the different plans by the other agencies, has aggravated the issue (Murched et al., 2015).

Lebanon also has a disaster management program that dates to the 1970s, known as the High Relief Committee (HRC), a governmental institution which is responsible for disaster response. This Committee is directly linked to the Office of the Prime Minister (Abou Zaki, 2010). The establishment of the High Relief Commission was a long process, yet it has no decision-making authority.

However, this committee was criticized throughout its management for different disasters and was accused of lacking the political will and support from ministers (Shearer & Pickup, 2007).

While in Lebanon many disaster management policies and laws were passed, all these remain without implementation.

During the first decade of the twentieth century, in 2002, the government passed Law 444, which established the National Council for the Environment that would take preventive measures against natural environmental disasters. In 2004, the government also passed Law 646, where every building of more than three stories would have to be designed to resist earthquakes.

With the development of many political events, the assassination of Prime Minister Rafik Hariri in 2005, the Israeli War in 2006, and the political deadlock that occurred in its aftermath, the government did not issue any decrees or laws concerning disaster management except Lebanon's National Strategy for Forest Fire Management that was established in 2007 (Haase, 2014).

In Lebanon, in terms of disaster management, attention is given to the response or recovery phase of a disaster from the local and international community. Conversely, no efforts are made in the mitigation and prevention phases, which are key phases in preventing the consequences of a disaster. To reduce disasters in Lebanon, the focus should be on both prevention of disasters and implementation of strategies.

Many constraints are preventing the Lebanese state from developing a clear strategic plan for disaster risk reduction: political, institutional, physical and human resources capacity, and gender-related constraints.

Political Constraints

The political system in Lebanon in addition to the divisions and the quota system is directly affecting the development of any holistic approach and plan for disaster risk reduction. Indeed, every ministry develops its own objectives without coordinating with other directorate generals or any other ministry (Murched et al., 2015). Moreover, this lack of information sharing and coordination between the ministries, the civil society, and the international players is challenging any plan for disaster risk reduction and even response (Murched et al., 2015).

Institutional Mechanism

The Lebanese population is extremely vulnerable to disasters. First, public administration is centralized in Lebanon, leaving peripheries and rural regions without any assistance compared to the capital, leading to huge gaps in the response and recovery from disasters. Second, the unplanned urban expansion, the lack of enforcement of buildings regulations for land use, and the various environmental factors have made the Lebanese population vulnerable to disasters (UNDP, 2015). Third, the various ministries do not coordinate their efforts, thus leading to duplication of efforts without a right plan for disaster mitigation (UNDP, 2015).

Lebanon lacks the establishment of a national platform to lead the country's disaster risk reduction and management plans; moreover, the High Relief Commission lacks the adequate tools to build a leading DRR plan; there is also the need to create a holistic institutional foundation for a clear disaster management plan. This institution should be responsible for policy-making and implementation, awareness raising, in addition to dissemination of early warning, and coordinating the emergency response and recovery. This plan was mentioned in priority 2 of the Sendai Framework for Disaster Risk Reduction: "Strengthening disaster risk governance to manage disaster risk".

Risk Information

In Lebanon, there is a lack of understanding of risk information to guide the plans of ministries and authorities toward, their developmental plans. Early warning mechanisms are still missing in Lebanon, in addition to the lack of community awareness about potential disasters affecting the preparedness for disasters. Clear disaster risk reduction plans are still missing in most of the ministries and local governments.

Capacity to Emergency Response

Lebanon lacks the physical capacity and human resources capacity to respond to any disaster, be it search and rescue, evacuation, firefighting, or medical first aid assistance. Moreover, local governments also lack the availability of firefighting and rescue equipment and machinery for emergency response. Moreover, the lack of availability of crisis operation rooms remains a big challenge when disasters strike.

Gender

Women still do not have access to opportunities in Lebanon; this makes them the most vulnerable when disasters strike.

While the High Relief Commission, the Lebanese Army, and the National Council for the Environment are the main governmental bodies responsible for disaster management, other bodies also take part in the relief process, mainly nongovernmental institutions, local governments, and municipality unions, thus the following section will expand on the role of these players in disaster management.

Nongovernmental Organizations in Lebanon

Disaster management strategies that have been established in Lebanon do not involve or include nongovernmental organizations, thus the role of these organizations remains limited (Moghniyeh et al., 2016). However, the ability of Lebanese society to respond to disasters relies on the organizations that fill gaps created by the absence of the state through providing the needed resources, especially the lack of communication and of the trust between the Lebanese population and the state hinders response to a disaster.

Disasters that have occurred in Lebanon, whether man-made or nature-made, have left lots of damages due to the lack of preparedness and the limited intervention of the state in the response. The mismanagement of resources and the absence of communication between ministries leave the response to disasters minimal. As argued in chapter 2, in the absence of the state, nonprofit organizations intervene in disaster response. To do so, these nonprofit organizations needed resources that were mainly provided from the diaspora (as remittances) or INGOs. Furthermore, international assistance in responding to disasters comes after calls from the government itself or from the population who ask for international assistance via social media by sharing the needs on the different platforms. In several disasters, Lebanon has asked for help from international entities, or international actors, whether international NGOs, states, diaspora, private sector, etc.

Throughout history, nongovernmental organizations in Lebanon have played a crucial role in recovery phases. For many people, these organizations provide the much-needed social, educational, health, and other services in areas where they are absent (Haddad, 2017, 2018; Haddad et al., 2019). In different instances throughout history, nongovernmental organizations have stepped in to replace the role of the failing state (Haddad, 2020). During disasters, the relationship was either cooperation or nonengagement where the government totally withdrew from the field.

These organizations have an extensive history in Lebanon: they existed even before the creation of the modern state of Lebanon. To date, there is an absence of information on the total number of associations that are functioning in Lebanon (Haddad, 2017). Many have estimated that the number of operational organizations in Lebanon totals between 5,000 and 6,000 (Haddad et al., 2018).

These organizations have played a crucial role in the history of Lebanon and in many instances were shaped by the social and political backgrounds of the state (Haddad, 2020). While these organizations had different relationships with the state, being cooperative, complementary, or co-optations, in many instances in the history, these organizations took the role of the state in replacing its services. With the outbreak of the Lebanese Civil War, the nature and activities of these organizations changed. Lebanon's infrastructure was destroyed, and the state and its administration totally shut down (Haddad, 2018).

This Civil War led to the total paralysis of the different public social welfare institutions that were established in the 1960s. Thus, confessional groups in most of the Lebanese religious communities developed social welfare programs and flourished in the social provision sector (Harik, 1994;

Traboulsi, 2007; Haddad, 2018). The flourishing of this sector was not based on encouragement from the government but on its inability to exercise any authority over their activities. Prior to and during the Civil War, the Lebanese government did not provide services to the poorest rural areas in the country, nor did it initiate public projects in the suburbs of the capital, hence freezing the institutions of the state. Due to the weakness and the unequal regional development policies, many suburban areas in the capital city, which became strongholds for rural migrants, were neglected.

These organizations were the first to respond to the state emergency and focused on community and local basis services such as providing food, medication, reconstruction, etc. With the failure of the state, many associations were created, and these benefited from financial assistance that poured into the state from western countries: thus, in most of the times these organizations competed over the sources of international funding (Haddad et al., 2019; Haddad, 2020).

Indeed, the absence of the state led to the development of community-based organizations and more than 550 organizations were officially created and registered at the Ministry of Interior (Haddad, 2017;2018; Haddad et al., 2019; Haddad, 2020). While it is crucial to point that many other organizations functioned without any official registration, these associations were indeed functioning in the absence of any governing laws.

The July 2006 war on Lebanon resulted in severe damages to the private and public infrastructure and a complete degradation of the economy. By the time of cessation of hostilities, nearly 1,200 people had died and about 4,400 were injured. About a quarter of Lebanon's population was displaced during, and around 500,000 people had their houses destroyed or damaged. Furthermore, the areas that were mostly affected were the same areas that traditionally witnessed the highest rates of marginalization from the state (Murshed, 2015). In 2006, it was once again these organizations that stepped in to assist displaced people (Haddad, 2018). Organizations from all over Lebanon opened their doors and gathered funds to assist the people. These organizations were successful in assisting in the relief phase mainly because most actors were international NGOs that came to Lebanon specifically to assist the communities.

In 2012, after the influx of Syrian refugees in Lebanon, strong sectarian clashes took place between two districts in Tripoli, Beb el Tebenne and Jabal Mohsen, leaving a high number of dead and injured. This crisis affected the health care sector in Tripoli, where access to health care became difficult with the ongoing clashes. Several NGOs and INGOs intervened to help the injured in both districts. One of the INGOs that stepped in was "Médecins sans Frontière" (MSF), which was the only organization, by November 2012, to have a health care unit in Jabal Mohsen. In April 2013,

MSF opened a clinic in Beb el Tebenne (Médecins sans Frontières). The only response from the Lebanese government to this conflict was to enforce the presence of the Lebanese Army. However, the containment of the violent and armed activities was not effective and INGOs were the only entities providing medical support.

It was no surprise that following the Beirut explosion associations in Lebanon were the first one to step in to assist. Associations from all over Lebanon altered their missions and combined their efforts to support the affected population. Since day one of the aftermath, associations cleaned the streets of glass and debris and provided food and shelter and medical aid for the most affected areas. Associations joined efforts to work under one umbrella to ensure that the people received the required assistance. Most active organizations post-explosion consisted of local associations. In addition, all international aid directed toward Lebanon was channeled either through the Lebanese Army or the NGOs since donors lost trust in the government and opted to directly assist these active associations. While more than 400 organizations registered with the Lebanese Army, stating their interest in helping in post-reconstructions, many others refused to do so (Fawaz, 2020).

From those organizations that stepped-up, there were organizations that were already focused on relief and reconstruction. However, other newer organizations shifted their focus to assist in reconstruction efforts. While these organizations were the first to step in, the lack of coordination and planning led to the failure of the response to the disaster. Indeed, this bottom-up approach to the management of the issue was obstructed with failure (Fawaz, 2020). A couple of months after the explosion, the area did not recover, and people are still homeless. Many have argued that the relief process was not successful. While working on their own with a total absence of the state, associations in Lebanon were alone in responding to the disaster. In fact, the lack of cooperation and funding led to the failure in reconstructing the city, and as such, a structural reform is highly needed in this sector.

Conclusion

This chapter analyzed the Beirut explosion and the mismanagement of the crisis through the lenses of disaster management and corruption, in the light of the presence of a strong civil society. It argues that four different factors affected the response of the state: failure of the bureaucracy, lack of a presence of clear disaster management strategy at the national level, economic crisis that led to increasing poverty rates, and the lack of cooperation from the side of civil society. To have a clear mitigation strategy, a holistic and participatory approach should be adopted. The level of corruption should be reduced, economic strategy should be adopted, and civil society should be included in the national disaster strategy. Only then will the Lebanese state be able to have a holistic approach to disaster management and response.

References

AbouAssi, K., Nabatchi, T., & Antoun, R. (2013). Citizen participation in public administration: Views from Lebanon. *International Journal of Public Administration*, *36*(14), 1029–1043. https://doi.org/10.1080/01900692.2013.809585.

Adwan, C. (2004). *Corruption in reconstruction: The cost of national consensus in post-war Lebanon*. Center for International Private Enterprise, Washington, December.

Ahmad Al-Qarioti, M. Q., & Al-Enezi, A. (2004). Organizational commitment of managers in Jordan: A field study. *International Journal of Public Administration*, *27*(5), 331–352.

Atzili, B. (2010). State weakness and "vacuum of power" in Lebanon. *Studies in Conflict and Terrorism*, *33*(8 (July)), 757–782. Https://doi.org/10.1080/105761 0X.2010.494172

Bachir, I. (1997). *Civil service reforms in Lebanon*. Beirut, Lebanon: American University of Beirut.

Bhuiyan, S., & Farazmand, A. (2020). Society and public policy in the Middle East and North Africa. *International Journal of Public Administration*, *43*(5), 373–377.

Bogaards, M. (2019). Formal and informal consociational institutions: A comparison of the national pact and the Taif agreement in Lebanon. *Nationalism and Ethnic Politics*, *25*(1), 27–42.

Crow, R. E., & Iskandar, A. (1961). Administrative reform in Lebanon 1958–1959. *International Review of Administrative Sciences*, *27*(3), 293–307.

El-Saad, F. (2001). *Strategy for the reform and development of public administration in Lebanon*. Beirut, Lebanon: Office of the Minister of State for Administrative Reform.

El-Zein, F., & Sims, H. (2004). Reforming war's administrative rubble in Lebanon. *Public Administration and Development: The International Journal of Management Research and Practice*, *24*(4), 279–288. https://doi.org/10.1002/ (issn)1099-162x.

Fawaz, T. (2007). *A history of modern Lebanon*. London: Pluto.

Ghosn, F., & Khoury, A. (2011). Lebanon after the civil war: Peace or the illusion of peace? *Middle East Journal*, *65*(3), 381–397.

Haase, T. W. (2014). Beyond the Hyogo framework: Disaster management in the Republic of Lebanon. In *Disaster and development*, edited by N. Kapucu and K. T. Liou (pp. 129–148). Switzerland: Springer International Publishing.

Haase, T. W. (2018). A challenging state of affairs: Public administration in the Republic of Lebanon. *International Journal of Public Administration*, *41*(10), 792–806.https://doi.org/10.1080/01900692.2017.1387148.

Haase, T. W., Haddad, T., & El-Badri, N. (2018). Public administration higher education in Lebanon: An investigation into the substance of advertised courses. *Journal of Public Affairs Education, 24*(1), 43–65.

Haddad, T. (2017). Analyzing state–civil society associations relationship: The case of Lebanon. *Voluntas: International Journal of Voluntary and Nonprofit Organizations, 28*(4), 1742–1761.

Haddad, T. (2018). Confrontation, co-optation, and cooperation civil society in postwar Lebanon. In R. Marchetti (Ed.), *Government–NGO relationships in Africa, Asia, Europe, and MENA* (pp. 235–252). New York: Routledge.

Haddad, T. (2017). Analysing state–civil society associations relationship: The case of lebanon. *VOLUNTAS: International Journal of Voluntary and Nonprofit Organizations, 28*(4), 1742–1761.

Haddad, T., Haase, T. W., & Ajamian, M. (2018). Religion, relief and reform: The history of civil society in Lebanon. In *Religion and civil society in the arab world* (pp. 128–159).

Haddad, T. (2020). Religious welfare organizations, citizenship, and the state in Lebanon. *Nonprofit Policy Forum, 11*(3), pp. 20190040.

Haddad, T., Haase, T. W., & Ajamian, M. (2019). Religion, relief and reform: The history of civil society in Lebanon. In T. Haddad & E. El Hindi (Eds.), *Religion and civil society in the Arab world: In the vortex of globalization and tradition* (pp. 128–159). New York: Routledge.

Harik, J. (1994). *The public and social services of the Lebanese militias. Vol. 14.* Oxford: Centre for Lebanese Studies.

Hassan, M. K., & Sarker, A. E. (2012). Managerial innovations in the Egyptian public health sector: An empirical investigation. *International Journal of Public Administration, 35*(11), 760–771.

Hatem, T. (1994). Egypt: Exploring management in the Middle East. *International Studies of Management & Organization, 24*(1–2), 116–136.

Iles, P., Almhedie, A., & Baruch, Y. (2012). Managing HR in the middle east: Challenges in the public sector. *Public Personnel Management, 41*(3), 465–492.

Jawad, R. (2009). Religion and social welfare in Lebanon: Treating the causes or symptoms of poverty? *Journal of Social Policy, 38*(1), 141–156.

Jreisat, J. (1970). Administrative change of local authorities: Lessons from four Arab countries. *Journal of Comparative Administration, 2*(2), 161–183.

Jreisat, J. E. (1989). Bureaucracy and development in Jordan. *Journal of Asian and African Studies, 24*(1–2), 94–105.

Jreisat, J. E. (1990). Administrative change and the Arab manager. *Public Administration and Development, 10*(4), 413–421.

Jreisat, J. E. (1999). Administrative reform and the Arab world economic growth. *Review of Policy Research, 16*(2), 19–40.

Jreisat, J. E. (2006). The Arab world: Reform or stalemate. *Journal of Asian and African Studies, 41*(5–6), 411–437.

Kisirwani, M.(2000) Accountability of Lebanese civil servants: An overview of disciplinary mechanisms. *Lebanon beyond* (pp. 103–124).

Makdisi, S., Kiwan, F., & Marktanner, M. (2010). Lebanon: The constrained democracy and its national impact. *Democracy in the Arab world: Explaining the deficit* (pp. 115–141).

Mehanna, K. (1993). *The role of civil society associations in disaster management: Experiences from the war.* Lebanon: Ministry of Health and Ministry of Social Affairs.

Murched, Z., Abilmona, F., & Zaarour, N. (2015). *Strengthening disaster risk management capacities in Lebanon-phase III.* Lebanon: UNDP.

Murshed, Z. (2015). *Strengthening disaster risk management capacities in Lebanon.* Outcome Evaluation Report 2009–2014. Beirut: United Nations Development Program.

Nakib, K., & Palmer, M. (1976). Traditionalism and change among Lebanese bureaucrats. *International Review of Administrative Sciences, 42*(1), 15–22.

Office of the Minister of State for Administrative Reform (OMSAR). (2011). *Strategy for the reform and development of public administration in Lebanon.* Beirut, Lebanon: Office of the Minister of State for Administrative Reform.

Parle, W. M., & Kisirwani, M. (1987). Assessing the impact of the post-civil war period on the Lebanese bureaucracy: A view from inside. *Journal of Asian and African Studies, 22*(1–2), 17–32. https://doi.org/10.1177/002190968702200102.

Safa, O. (2010). Lebanon. In J. Dizzard, C. Walker & S. Cook (Eds.), *Countries at the crossroads: An analysis of democratic governance* (pp. 341–360). New York: Freedom House.

Salamey, I. (2014). *The government and politics of Lebanon.* New York: Routledge.

Shearer, D., & Pickup, F. (2007). Still falling short: Protection and partnerships in the Lebanon emergency response. *Disasters, 31*(4), 336–352.

Transparency International. (2020). Corruption Perception Index. https://www.transparency.org/en/cpi/2020.

UNDP. (2015). Launching of the crisis operation room - Lebanon. *ReliefWeb.* https://reliefweb.int/report/lebanon/launching-crisis-operation-room.

4 The Role of International Players in the Response and Recovery from the Beirut Port Explosion

Introduction

Since its independence, Lebanon's administrative model was based on a sectarian power-sharing system that led the state to become part of a regional and international power struggle for domination. All these international state players viewed the Beirut explosion as an opportunity to play a role in Lebanon. Indeed, this event changed the political landscape in Lebanon and increased foreign intervention in the state, mirroring long-standing foreign power rivalries over Lebanon.

After the Beirut explosion, Lebanon lacked the basic resources needed for reconstruction and relief efforts, and heavily relied on external support for reconstruction. International powers started developing proposals for Lebanon that varied from economic aid to reconstruction. However, the Lebanese political system, tainted with corruption, hindered all international efforts to help the state. In addition to highlighting high levels of division present in the Lebanese government, the explosion also highlighted the failure of the government to provide basic needs for its citizens, especially in times of emergency. This explosion also shed light on the failed Lebanese political structure that is based on confessional power sharing and is unsuited for a modern state.

In addition, this crisis presented a new dimension in the architecture of international aid to Lebanon. Local NGOs received funds from outside sources, including the Lebanese diaspora or international humanitarian organizations, some of whom directly intervened to respond to the blast. Linking this response to the literature reviewed in Chapter 1, this chapter will analyze how international assistance and foreign aid are conditioned by strategic, political, diplomatic, and geostrategic reasons and are dominated by economic concerns. Based on interviews with experts in international relations theories and civil society actors involved in direct response on the ground, this chapter will further analyze the role played by each of

DOI: 10.4324/9781003222545-5

the different international players and their impact on Lebanese citizens. It will review the ways the international order handled the vulnerability of the state and how responding to the event reproduced power sharing at the international level. It will argue that international response to the explosion was indeed shaped by global factors, and humanitarian assistance varied between different players: the assistance, and sometimes lack of assistance, by the international community highlighted the weaknesses of the state and undermined its credibility.

Methodology

To understand the role of international players in disaster response and their relationship with the state, we conducted interviews with associations and initiatives that responded post-explosion. Qualitative data were collected through a series of semi-structured interviews (Krueger & Casey, 2015). The interviewees were experts in international relations theories or were involved in direct response on the ground and were active in disaster response since day one of the aftermath of the explosion. All interviews were conducted during the months of September and October 2021 (Appendix 1 presents the list of interviewees and their main research focuses).

The interviews were recorded, translated, and transcribed into separate documents and were thematically coded and analyzed using MaxQDA (Saldana, 2013; Haase et al., 2018). Given the difficulties in collecting valid data in Middle Eastern contexts (Clark, 2006; Haase et al., 2018), we used purposeful sampling in the selection of participants (Cresswell & Clark, 2011). The participants were asked semi-structured questions about (1) the role of international players in disaster response, (2) the reasons behind this intervention, and (3) the long-term effect of this intervention. Interviews were capped at 15 as they encompassed a broad range of perspectives that helped grasp theoretical saturation in respect to the concepts and themes that emerged (Corbin & Strauss, 2014). Each interview was structured around the same five questions: (1) What was the role of international players in response to the Beirut Port explosion? (2) What strategies did they use? (3) What was the economic and social impact of these interventions? (4) Why did they intervene? (5) What are the lessons learned?

Findings

Findings were divided into four main categories: (1) the role of international humanitarian organizations, (2) the role of states, (3) the role of the diaspora, and (4) the impact of the intervention.

International Community

As a direct response to the explosion, international humanitarian organizations stepped in to assist and provide relief. These organizations played a major role in the disaster relief progress on the ground. The first of such players was the United Nations. The first International Search and Rescue Advisory Group (INSARAG) team, a global network of more than 90 countries and organizations working under the United Nations umbrella, arrived 24 hours after the explosion. In the first days and weeks of the response, the teams coordinated search-and-rescue operations and provided critical coordination support to the Lebanese government. These teams also supported in the assessment of structural damages and detected hazardous material and assisted local communities and businesses to resume their services (Renino, 2020).

The United Nations, along with other partners, launched an appeal to mobilize $565 million for psychological support in addition to response and recovery services provided through its different agencies: it created an Emergency Operations Centre (EOC) under the UN Office for the Coordination of Humanitarian Affairs (OCHA). Moreover, an expert group of 19 members from the UN Disaster Assessment and Coordination (UNDAC) team analyzed the situation on the field and assisted in the coordination of the emergency relief activities on the ground. Concurrently, the World Food Program (WFP) worked on logistical supplies to ensure that the port remained operational in addition to securing food parcels for over 150,000 people affected by the blast (The Borgen Project, 2020). The UNICEF also sent members to distribute medical supplies and hygiene kits. Moreover, in the post-disaster phase, the UN with the assistance of the EU launched a Rapid Damage and Needs Assessment (RDNA). This assessment concluded that the damage value was between $3.8 and $4.6 billion, while financial losses were between $2.9 and $3.5 billion. Based on the study, the impact of the disaster affected mainly key sectors vital for growth, such as housing, tourism, and commerce (World Bank, 2021).

In addition to the United Nations, many international NGOs stepped in to assist in the response phase. For example, the British Red Cross managed an emergency fund for medical assistance in cooperation with the Lebanese Red Cross. "Humanity and Inclusion", an American NGO dispatched 100 members to assist in the rehabilitation. The Islamic Relief USA created a supply chain for emergency aid, Project HOPE focused on distributing emergency health kits, and the International Rescue Committee focused on providing cash aid to the ones affected, in addition to funding local NGOs that focused on mental health (https://borgenproject.org/eight-organizations -who-provided-aid-after-the-explosion-in-beirut-aradia-webb/).

From the international community's point of view, this intervention was humanitarian and did not have any political agenda attached to it. As explained by Interviewee 1: "I think it was purely a humanitarian approach to try to support the Lebanese people, but I don't think anybody had a plan or a political agenda in that sense they were pushing" (Interviewee 1, 2021). This sentiment was also stressed by Interviewee 2 who argued: "At this humanitarian level, the response was positive in the sense that the world did not leave Lebanon, that the world did not neglect the victims of the explosion" (Interviewee 2, 2021).

The findings also showed that the international community did not have a clear strategy in their response efforts. The community's only concern was not to send relief support to the state but to organizations working on the field: "I don't think they had any strategy" (Interviewee 1, 2021). As for the type of support, it started with medical related relief: "Most international assistance coming from the international community started with building field hospitals and sending medications" (Interviewee 2, 2021).

The international community's main concern was not to directly support the government but to provide relief support to the people on the ground: "I think the only guideline was not to send money to the government but to try to send money directly to trusted organizations" (Interviewee 1, 2021). This point was also supported by Interviewee 2: "They knew that they could not trust Lebanese officials" (Interviewee 2, 2021). This mistrust was mainly caused by the government as it did not have the right capacity or did not know how to respond to the damage caused by the explosion. "The government did not have the capacity, nor the resources to do serious cleanup, and serious caretaking of the consequences" (Interviewee 1, 2021). The corrupt practices of the Lebanese government were highlighted in this support: "in the sense that no money should come to the Lebanese Government without serious reforms that remain the case. And that is why they directed any funds that they have to civil society rather than with the government" (Interviewee 1, 2021).

Most of the INGOs preferred to cooperate with local partners and NGOs.

We adopt a community-based approach, and all our programs are implemented through local partners. We do collaborate with INGOs, but implementation is mainly conducted through local partners. Not only did we did collaborate with local NGOs, but also with private sector actors.

(Interviewee 12, 2021)

Competition over funding was also highlighted and revealed that there was a huge competition between NGOs on the ground over international funds, and this in turn negatively influenced the coordination between different players (Interviewee 13, 2021) and affected the quality of work conducted on the field:

> Competition was high as donors from outside have a high budget for Lebanon. This competition affected the quality of the services on the ground because many organizations changed their mission just to get access to international assistance.
>
> (Interviewee 13, 2021)

Moreover, and as argued by Interviewee 10 (2021), local NGOs had to create visibility of their work on the field to attract more funding: "We learned that the more quickly you act, the more you are present on the ground, the more you can have funding".

The absence of the state was a highlight in the findings as this affected the work on the ground:

> The government was far from the main corps of the plan. It was present in the meetings but was not the main/base actor who distributed tasks. In disasters, the entity that should provide a sense of order on the ground is the government; that was not the case during the response to the Beirut Explosion.
>
> (Interviewee 13, 2021)

EU and World Bank

Both the World Bank and the European Union played a crucial role in the disaster response to the explosion. As stressed by Interviewee 6 (2021), international organizations were faced with three different options: rely on the corrupt government to channel disbursement; maintain control over the funding decision, risking criticism from foreign influence; or not assisting altogether. As such, a new model labeled "Reform, Recovery and Reconstruction Framework" (3Rs) was presented.

This model was launched four months after the blast by the EU, the UN, and the World Bank. This framework was defined as "a people-centered recovery and reconstruction framework focusing on a period of 18 months that will bridge the immediate humanitarian response and the medium-term recovery and reconstruction efforts to put Lebanon on a path of sustainable development" (Arab Reform Initiative, 2021). This report stressed on the need for institutional reform to assist the state, which varied between macroeconomic stabilization, governance measures, and establishing a proper environment for the private sector (Geha, 2021).

This framework was developed to ensure funds were distributed properly. The main aim was to pool all donations into a system with a suitable structure empowering civil society by channeling funds directly toward nongovernmental organizations. Based on the framework presented, once launched, the Lebanese organizations would be part of the steering committee governing the funds and would have a crucial role in monitoring the implementation (Interviewee 6, 2021). As for the Lebanese government, this latter would hold a seat in the governing body, as its access to long-term recovery funds was subjected to the introduction of administrative and economic reforms. As per Interviewee 8 (2021), this framework was a step toward reimagining international support that empowered people and civil society in targeted countries. However, the main concern was that aid and investments were directly linked to the Lebanese government and whether they would act on the fiscal, financial, social, and governance reforms (World Bank, 2021).

However, as stressed by Interviewees 7 and 8 (2021), the restrictions placed in return altered relief efforts. Indeed, as highlighted in the findings, one of the major concerns for working on the ground were the restrictions placed by the international community and mainly the 3Rs:

> What I know is that on the international plan we are working because of the presence of 3Rs. It is one of the conditions. It's been a year since we have been trying to convince the international community not to link humanitarian aid with reforms because Lebanese people need help, and some are really at poverty rate. We cannot link humanitarian aid to reform and wait for the money, while people are in need. According to the latest number of the World Bank, 60% or more are under the limit of poverty.
>
> (Interviewee 10, 2021)

Role Played by the States

After less than two days post-explosion, many regional and international state actors stepped in to assist in the relief process: Russia and Iran, in addition to other regional actors, such as Egypt, Iraq, Jordan, Morocco, Qatar, and Turkey, having interests or ties in Lebanon stepped in, and established field hospitals and relief centers (Renino, 2020). The United States, through the USAID agency, pledged US$17 million for disaster response. Italy also contributed to sending funds and medical and food supplies. These aids were directly delivered to UN agencies, NGOs, and hospitals as opposed to sending them to the government (Renino, 2020).

Here the role differed with the states. While western states played a major role, regional ones had a more limited role. "The Arabs of course did not do anything; they did not propose themselves as candidates of the solution which was a role that historically they used to do. Qatar, Doha in 2008 they did not do anything" (Interviewee 4, 2021).

As presented by the findings, for the first time, regional states and countries did not fully intervene in the response phase. Interviewee 5 (2021) stated that "it seems the Gulf countries have not come forward much. They set up hospitals, humanitarian aid but did not play a political role". This type of intervention was compared to other interventions where Arab states played a crucial and major role whenever a disaster would strike in Lebanon. For example, in 2006, regional states were directly involved in the full response and reconstruction.

This time, Arab states did not really invest in the response. As clearly stated by Interviewee 2 (2021):

> The big difference was that Gulf countries who really placed heavy weights after the 2006 War were completely absent after Beirut Port Explosion. This absence was mainly because these states had different political agendas and Lebanon was not a priority.

Indeed, as argued by Interviewee 1 (2021), "a political decision, of course, they took a collective decision to not support Lebanon". This claim was supported by Interviewee 5, (2021), who argued that the Gulf states played a humanitarian role that was minimal compared with other disasters:

> It was obvious that the political boycott had an impact. You can compare these recent reactions to the Israeli attacks of 2006. The Arab world and the Gulf States, Qatar, Saudi Arabia, Kuwait, the United Arab Emirates, intervened automatically in 2006, they paid. After the port disaster, even their humanitarian aid was little and very basic.
>
> (Interviewee 5, 2021)

Indeed, Arab states' involvement was more humanitarian and medical. Qatar, Kuwait, and UAE, all intervened to provide medical support and emergency relief (Interviewee 3, 2021). However, this assistance was not as significant as it had been previously. Indeed, Interviewees stressed that this nonintervention was due to political reasons. Interviewee 4 (2021) analyzed the role played by Saudi Arabia and linked this nonintervention to two major reasons: the first was political and the second related to internal politics:

> Arabs did not intervene because Saudi Arabia, who was a major actor in Lebanese politics for years and years, has given up. They are less

engaged specifically for two reasons. In my opinion, Saudi Arabia should not invest anymore in Lebanon. The second reason is that they have their own internal challenges with Mohammad Ben Salman, so they preferred to refocus their energy in their own politics to a greater extent.

(Interviewee 4, 2021)

The lack of support from Saudi Arabia occurred because of two major political reasons: the first was due to the lack of trust in the Lebanese government as it was ranked 137 out of 198 countries in Transparency International's Corruption Perceptions Index. Thus, there was a lack of transparency in dealing with funds, and the second being the intentional intervention of the regional and international players to increase their presence and power in the complex Lebanese political game (Renino, 2020).

French Role

The role of the French state was highlighted in the interviews; indeed, the French were among the first states to intervene in the relief efforts in Lebanon. On August 5, one day after the explosion, France sent two military planes containing 18 tons of medical equipment and 700 tons of food, and doctors and relief workers were also sent.

President Macron showed up two days after the explosion, visited Lebanon twice in one month. He helped with the explosion, from sending military teams to trying to understand and investigate what happened and to alleviate the consequences.

(Interviewee 2, 2021)

Macron sent Lebanese leaders a road map that stated the financial and political changes required to encourage foreign aid assistance. During his second visit to Lebanon, he provided a 15-day time frame for Lebanese politicians to assign a new cabinet. In addition to the international conference he held, President Macron announced that two conferences would be held to assist in the reconstruction aid and to build international support for the reform agenda. This initiative presented by the French president was faced with questions about the effectiveness of such a move, especially because of the regional US–Iran rivalry.

Indeed, all interviewees stressed on the humanitarian and political role played by the French state. From the humanitarian standpoint, and as Interviewee 2 (2021) stressed, the French reacted as if the disaster happened on their own territory:

France and the French President took a real initiative and behaved as if the explosion occurred on French territory, affecting French people. In that sense, in a very responsible way in a very responsive way.

(Interviewee 2, 2021)

This contribution by the French government was based on the historical relationship between Lebanon and the French state:

In that sense, there has been a special link between Mount Lebanon and France since the 13th century. According to many scholars, there is a special link with France, from the period of the mandate, which expanded and strengthened the connection. Many Lebanese again, I am sure you are familiar with the term, refer to France as Lebanon's merciful mother.

(Interviewee 2, 2021)

French interference took on a political stance, as President Macron launched an initiative to activate the Lebanese government.

Politically, Macron launched a very important initiative to activate a Lebanese government to bring to the table different Lebanese leaders who could not agree on their own, to agree and to promise them international help.

(Interviewee 2, 2021)

After the Beirut blast, on August 9, France co-organized with the United Nations in an international conference for international aid for Lebanon. This event was attended by world leaders and government officials, whereby 36 countries pledged $300 million for emergency support. Macron's program listed four sectors in need of immediate attention: humanitarian aid and a response to the COVID-19 pandemic, physical reconstruction from the blast, political and economic reforms, and early parliamentary elections. The conference also called for the immediate resumption of talks with the IMF for loans and swift moves to fight graft. In parallel, the White House also called for transparency, reform, and accountability.

Politically, this interference was based on two different projects, first to reaffirm the importance of Lebanon to the French state:

France wanted to use the opportunity to establish two things, first of all, to reconfirm that Lebanon means a lot to it, and that it wants to play a leading role in Lebanon, especially at a time where Americans were withdrawing, or were not really pushing for a major role for themselves. (Interviewee 1, 2021)

The second, being more regional and asserting, the French role as a major player in the region. This intervention was viewed by many as French mainly because of the latter's only remaining influence in the region.

Second, which is closely connected is to play a role with Iran where Iran and the US were not speaking to each other. I think they use the occasion to benefit French interests predominantly also, to get back in on the political scene in Lebanon in that sense.

(Interviewee 1, 2021)

To evaluate this intervention, many viewed it as a failure on the long term. This failure was mainly due to two reasons: the first was that the project was not very well grounded and analyzed, and the second was due to the resistance of the ruling class to any project introduced by the French. This was portrayed by Interviewee 4 (2021) who argued:

You have the political initiative that Macron started which did not really reflect an international initiative but as a European state, in this case France. Macron came to Lebanon and tried to impose himself as the main mediator to the Lebanese crisis. Usually, this failure is blamed on the ruling class, as they did not respond to the initiative. In fact, this is not only the case, and it does not explain the failure. His initiative was not well grounded, and we made a lot of mistakes, so the failure is the failure of Macron himself.

Diaspora

The third international player in this disaster response was the Lebanese diaspora. The Lebanese diaspora is present all over the world and played a crucial role in the disaster response. Indeed, they created networks for assistance connected to each other. This intervention was seen by many as normal since it was emotional, mental, and political.

It is very normal and very expected, and it was amazing. As usual, the Lebanese still have that huge connection, emotional and mental and political connection to Lebanon and they would really jump in to help on any occasion they can. We saw a huge number of initiatives by individuals and communities and churches and mosques and all kinds of initiatives that were really making a difference and were able to gather money and make a difference on small scales of course, but very significant. All this power is still there and should be used in the right way. But these people need somebody to trust so they can work with and need the state that they trust so they can invest them.

(Interviewee 1, 2021)

The Lebanese diaspora includes Lebanese residing in foreign countries, prominent professionals who developed funds via their NGOs or crowdfunding. In addition, celebrities and popular figures organized events to raise funds and donations to the affected population. It is not the first time that the Lebanese diaspora feels the need to help its population. After the Civil War, the Lebanese diaspora filled the gap and assisted in the response and the reconstruction of the affected and damaged areas by sending donations.

After August 4, 2020, a coalition between NGOs founded by Lebanese diaspora and registered outside Lebanon was formed and resulted in opening the "Beirut Emergency Fund 2020". This fund was launched by Life Lebanon, an NGO that brought together Lebanese professionals around the globe (May Nasrallah, 2020). Moreover, the diaspora assisted Lebanon by organizing charity diners, auctions, or events. Life Lebanon organized a "Solidarity dinner" in London which resulted in $1.7 million dollars in donations (May Nasrallah, 2020/13). Impact Lebanon, which is a nonprofit organization based in the United Kingdom but founded by Lebanese, donated around $9.2 million dollars to NGOs in Lebanon to assist in the response to the explosion (Ollie Williams, 2021/15). Donations were collected not only by the Lebanese diaspora, but also by corporations, businessmen, and citizens who took part in the response to the explosion. Sotheby's, an American multinational corporation based in New York City, prominent in the fine art and decoration sector, organized a charity auction "To Beirut with Love" which resulted in a donation of over US$300,000.

Celebrities and social media influencers took part in the response to the Beirut Port explosion. In fact, celebrities with Lebanese roots organized events to collect donations and in commemoration of the victims of the explosion. Mika, a British-Lebanese singer residing in France, donated over $1.1 million to the Lebanese Red Cross and Save the Children after organizing the "I love Beirut" concert (Save the Children, September 2020). Donations to this concert were collected via ticket sales, donations on GoFundMe, a social media fundraising platform, and sponsors.

The French Lebanese trumpeter and musician Ibrahim Maalouf organized a concert "Unis pour le Liban" at the Olympia in France on October 1, 2020, to raise donations to rebuild Beirut (France 24/18). This concert was streamed on French televisions TV5 Monde and France 24 and was sponsored by Ibrahim

Maalouf, who performed with several international and French artists at the Olympia (UNESCO – 1/10/2020). The concert was preceded by a documentary as part of the "envoyé special" program showing the devastating explosion (France 24/18). UNESCO joined this concert and accepted donations (UNESCO 1/102020). This event raised around €2 million in France, and Ibrahim Maalouf continued his support by joining the Beirut Chant Festival and performing before Christmas (Alaa Kanaan – 5/12/2020/17).

Evaluation and Lessons Learned

As for lessons learned from this disaster and international interventions, it was clear that every intervention was based on certain political considerations. Every international player had a certain political or personal interest in the intervention.

> The lesson is that there is no support, like free value support from the international community. They have their own interest in Lebanon no matter how the Lebanese see it. They have their personal interest, and they will do everything in respect to that interest.
>
> (Interviewee 7, 2021)

Moreover, as an evaluation, this intervention was viewed as negative:

> When we look back at it, I think it was a very negative interference, because it did not push in the right direction or for stabilization. Stabilization was with all the wrong actors and on the wrong places, instead of pushing for serious actual change that was and would have been possible after the explosion.

To have a proper intervention and response, the presence of a state to coordinate all the response efforts is required:

> The first lesson learned is that we need a state in Lebanon. the public bureaucracy in Lebanon spreads out responsibilities over every aspect of decision making to the extent that no one become responsible. There is a need of an entity that coordinates all these different efforts.
>
> (Interviewee 5, 2021)

The second lesson was that corruption undermines any intervention:

> This is another lesson: this is part of the rampant corruption practices where you cannot point fingers at anyone as responsible and this is

part of the confessional constructed bureaucracy. Lebanese citizens are not safe as long as there is no rule of law to be utilized equally among all Lebanese and these dangerous and community threatening warehouses are everywhere in the country, and they can explode at any time. As long as there is no government monitoring and no oversight, there is no practical rule of law utilized to protect our country's citizens. We are all vulnerable, and we can all be blown up in one way or another. Do you know the last lesson that shouldn't be known and may be relevant to your study? At the end of the day, no one will help Lebanese but Lebanese themselves, otherwise, international organizations have different agendas. These agendas may provide some support here and there, but such support is not necessarily linked to the Lebanese sustainable political future and therefore, unless Lebanese citizens come together to manage their own house, they will continue to be manipulated by foreign powers and their agendas, whether that comes from the east or the west.

(Interviewee 3, 2021)

Analysis

This study has highlighted the role played by each of the different players in disaster response in Lebanon. Linking these findings to the literature reviewed in Chapter 2, it is obvious that each of the international players had a different reason to intervene as international aid and assistance is based on strategic, political, and geostrategical concerns. The political scene in the Lebanese state directly affected the role of each player: none of the different players had trust in the Lebanese government and worked on finding new ways to assist in the relief process and bypassing as well as sometimes ignoring the role that the state should play.

Literature on international assistance provided by states argues that international assistance is multifaceted and considers the characteristics of the affected countries (Wei & Marinova, 2016). It is based on many factors such as the (1) socioeconomic development of the state concerned, the (2) political and diplomatic effect of the assistance, and (3) the economic benefit for the donor state, in addition to the geostrategies of the different parties involved (Wei et al., 2019).

When studying disaster response, it is important to address the political agendas and motivations of donor states to identify the conditions placed on donations, albeit sometimes unofficial, which are contrary to the principle of humanitarianism in this context. Thus, when responding to disasters donor states usually focus on maximizing their power in international relations (Morgenthau, 1978) (Zhang, 2006; Wei et al., 2014); the type of assistance from foreign actors is highly based on political and strategic considerations (Wei et al., 2019; Annen & Strickland, 2017; Zagefka & James, 2015). This section demonstrated that state intervention in international humanitarian response is not only based on pure humanitarian reasons. Indeed, decisions to respond and the level of response are highly contingent upon different strategic decisions and reasons.

Corruption of the state was a major factor in the response process: as argued in Chapter 2, when recipient states have weak institutions, donors usually direct their foreign aid toward both NGOs and multilateral organizations. Thus, the internal politics and corruption that tainted the Lebanese state were major factors in deciding on the type of assistance. States and humanitarian organizations either refused to provide direct assistance to the state or, on the other hand, demanded reform to initiate the assistance process. Moreover, many states were reluctant to play a major role in helping the Lebanese government due to geostrategic and political reasons; while the Arab states provided humanitarian relief and assistance, they were reluctant to play an additional role.

The major player was the French state; this intervention had both humanitarian and political considerations. Indeed, this intervention was linked to the historical political and social role of the French state in Lebanon. The history of French presence in Lebanon goes back to the 16th century and increased by the end of the 19th century when French missionaries started creating schools on Lebanese territory, and in 1875, they established the French university Saint Joseph that still exists until today. By the end of World War I, the League of Nations designated Lebanon as a French protectorate and assigned France as an administrator over Lebanon to steer the five provinces into self-governance. The main aim was to reach the independence of Lebanon as opposed to it becoming a French colony. Thus, between 1920 and 1943, Greater Lebanon was placed under French mandate until it reached its independence and was declared the Lebanese Republic, and France introduced the first Constitution in 1926. The mandate legacy included the development of French schools that graduated most of the country's elite.

Post-independence, the links between France and the Maronites started to weaken, and France's influence in the region started to decrease. Since then, the two countries have had close relations (Vohra, 2021). Indeed, France is always seen as a major economic partner of Lebanon; and the Lebanese diaspora in France is considered as the first Lebanese diaspora. There are around 23,000 French people in Lebanon and around 210,000 Lebanese people in France (Vohra, 2021). Moreover, a third of the population speaks the French language. In 2018, the French ambassador to Lebanon, Bruno Foucher, stated that Lebanon was the number one country outside France to teach the French curriculum (Vohra, 2021). In 2018, a donor's conference held in Paris collected around $13 billion. However, these funds were not delivered to Lebanon as the latter did not initiate the promised revisions and reform. At the domestic level, this interference gave the French player window to show the world the important role of France in the Eastern Mediterranean via the Lebanese gate, especially after the setback in the municipal elections, and the failure of the French Navy to inspect a Turkish ship heading to Libya. Indeed, this interference had social, political, and cultural dimensions. France used its soft power in the interference in Lebanon. At the political level, France realized that it could access the Mideast relations via Lebanon, ahistorically. Many viewed this interference as a neo-colonialist interference (Cook, 2020). The Lebanese population viewing France's involvement as that of a savior, and an online petition signed by 60,000 demanded the restoration of the French mandate. At the economic level, France focused on assisting Lebanon to manage the emergence and reconstruction funds; it also pushed leaders to reform the public sector and initiate the negotiation with the International Monetary Fund. Indeed, this conditional aid was paralleled with the threat of imposing sanctions on the elites if these did not implement the reforms suggested. At the cultural level, France highlighted cultural and historical ties with Lebanon during Macron's second visit to Beirut. This visit coincided with the centennial anniversary of "Greater Lebanon", and Macron engaged with protestors on the ground during his visit to Beirut as well as when visiting the renowned Lebanese singer Fairouz.

International Humanitarian Assistance

This chapter argued that while international humanitarian assistance should be directed toward helping individuals in emergency situations without any discrimination based on race, citizenship, or political considerations, the reality is different. Those organizations took into consideration the reality of politics in Lebanon and the high level of corruption in the state. While they wanted to assist in the relief process, they were reluctant to cooperate with the Lebanese government. This mistrust is why they directed their work to organizations working on the field, while also providing a road map for the Lebanese state to receive funding.

It is important to stress the role played by the EU. Since Lebanon is present on the Mediterranean Sea, any deterioration in Lebanese internal politics and security will directly affect the security of all the European states present on the other side of the sea. The EU was apprehensive that the deterioration of the situation in Lebanon would in turn lead to humanitarian issues and internal conflict leading to regional instability (Geha, 2021). Moreover, this interference was also linked to values of inclusivity and civil liberty that are historically present in Lebanon. Indeed, many local associations are partnering with the EU to spread these values. Thus, in its interference, the EU regarded the stability of the Lebanese state as advancing its own interest, especially in a region full of instability and turmoil (Geha, 2021).

Role of Diaspora

Throughout the years, relying on international players was a necessity to overcome crisis and fill gaps unsolved by the Lebanese state. The Lebanese diaspora has always played a key role in rescuing Lebanese residing in Lebanon by sending in kind donation or cash or by simply spreading the call in their country of residence. The response to the Beirut Port explosion was based on in-kind or cash donations from states, international NGOs, UN agencies, and Lebanese diaspora. The Lebanese diaspora, which is estimated to be three to four times bigger than the Lebanese population residing in Lebanon, played a major role in the response (France 24/11).

Indeed, as argued in Chapter 2, the diaspora played a crucial role in responding to the disaster in Lebanon. They proved to be an important player at the international level as they organized into groups and linked to each other throughout the world to support the Lebanese community. These diasporas ensured that the failure of the government was highlighted and emphasized the need to direct the assistance to the people and NGOs. They were among the first to mobilize and used social media to highlight the need for assistance and started organizing to secure funding for relief. However, as discussed in Chapter 2, while this support was quickly mobilized, it was mainly a short-term direct response, and the donations sent by the diaspora were not used in an effective way due to the absence of an effective channel for response in the affected community.

Conclusion

This chapter has argued that international assistance and foreign aid are mainly based on strategic, political, diplomatic, and geostrategic reasons and are dominated by economic concerns. International donors, mainly states, take into consideration their own benefits and agendas when responding to disasters; France played a crucial role linking it to social, cultural, and political reasons. Moreover, this chapter demonstrated how some international aid emphasized the failure of the affected governments in managing disasters and how the reliance on these international donors would lead to limited commitment on the part of the affected state and weak governance of local institutions.

Linking this part to the literature reviewed in Chapter 2, disaster responses are not independent from international relations. This chapter has shown that in developing contexts, disaster response is a functional cooperation that is used to advance the interest of different players. Different players emerged to fill in the gap left by the weak state. While, as argued in Chapter 2, the emergency relief responses of humanitarian organizations should be based on human rights and on the principle of "do no harm", and on impartiality, irrespective of economic or political purposes, this chapter illustrated that assistance is mostly based on strategic and political reasons and is usually dominated by economic concerns. This international assistance has highlighted the weakness of the Lebanese state that is tainted with corruption, linking foreign assistance with reform strategies, and directing the assistance to NGOs and actors providing support on the ground.

When it comes to disaster response in Lebanon, states' responses were based on political and strategic considerations. In this case, France focused on maximizing its regional power in the region. This chapter has illustrated that international assistance is more based on strategical than geographical proximity. However, this supply-driven reliance on international donors led to limited commitment from the state and disordered decision-making at the local level. A year after the explosion, Lebanon has witnessed a drop in the funding and organizations that are still working on rebuilding Beirut, who are facing difficulties in finishing their projects.

Chapter 5 will focus on the role of local players in disaster response and will analyze the reasons behind this failure.

Appendix 1: List of interviewees and their research focus

Interviewee	Area of Focus	Date
Interviewee 1	International Relations expert	September 2021
Interviewee 2	International Relations expert	September 2021
Interviewee 3	International Relations expert	October 2021
Interviewee 4	International Relations expert	September 2021
Interviewee 5	International Relations expert	September 2021
Interviewee 6	International Relations expert	October 2021
Interviewee 7	International Relations expert	October 2021
Interviewee 8	International Relations expert	September 2021
Interviewee 9	INGO staff	September 2021
Interviewee 10	INGO staff	October 2021
Interviewee 11	INGO staff	October 2021
Interviewee 12	INGO staff	October 2021
Interviewee 13	INGO program manager	October 2021
Interviewee 14	INGO staff	October 2021
Interviewee 15	INGO staff	October 2021

References

Creswell, J. W., & Plano Clark, V. L. (2011). *Designing and conducting mixed methods research* (2nd ed.). Los Angeles, CA: Sage Publications.

Corbin, J., & Strauss, A. (2014). *Basics of qualitative research* (3rd ed). Thousand Oaks, CA: Sage.

Haase, T. W., Haddad, T., & El-Badri, N. (2018). Public administration higher education in Lebanon: An investigation into the substance of advertised courses. *Journal of Public Affairs Education, 24*(1), 43–65.

Krueger, R. A., & Casey, M. A. (2015). *Focus groups: A practical guide for applied research.* Thousand Oaks, CA: Sage Publications.

Nakib, K., & Palmer, M. (1976). Traditionalism and change among Lebanese bureaucrats. *International Review of Administrative Sciences, 42*(1), 15–22.

Nasrallah, M. (2020). The role of the diaspora in healing Lebanon. *Executive Magazine.* Last modified October 28, 2020. https://www.executive-magazine. com/opinion/the-role-of-the-diaspora-in-healing-lebanon.

Renino, R. (2020). Beirut blast disaster response: International aid and grassroots mobilization. *Twai.* Last modified October 9, 2020. https://www.twai.it/journal /tnote-88/.

Saldana, J. (2013). *The coding manual for qualitative researchers* (2nd ed.). London: Sage.

The Borgen Project. (2020). 8 organizations helping after the explosion in Beirut. Last modified September 22, 2020. https://borgenproject.org/eight-organizations -who-provided-aid-after-the-explosion-in-beirut-aradia-webb/.

Vohra, A. (2021). Lebanon's failure is partly Macron's fault. *Foreign Policy.* Last modified June 23, 2021. https://foreignpolicy.com/2021/06/23/lebanons-failure- is-partly-macrons-fault/.

Williams, O. A. (2021). Where is Lebanon's diaspora today, one year after the Beirut Blast? *Forbes.* https://www.forbes.com/sites/oliverwilliams1/2021/08/04/where -are-lebanons-diaspora-today-one-year-after-the-beirut-blast/?sh=6798fbbe44ff.

World Bank. (2021). The World Bank in Lebanon. Last modified October 17, 2021. https://www.worldbank.org/en/country/lebanon/overview#1.

5 The Role of Local Actors in Disaster Response
August 4 Beirut Port Explosion

Introduction

The Beirut Port explosion took place during many compounding crises in Lebanon, mainly the Syrian crisis that led to the influx of more than 1.5 million Syrian refugees, in addition to an economic crisis that started in 2019 and the COVID-19 outbreak that strained the health system in the state. In addition to the international players that intervened in the response phase, many local players stepped in to help, from governmental institutions to NGOs and volunteers assisting on the ground. In this regard, this chapter assesses the role of the government, nonprofit associations, the Lebanese Army, and volunteers. Moreover, this chapter will analyze the effect of this intervention on the long-term disaster recovery in Lebanon.

In disaster management, it is important to assess the disaster response mechanisms adopted by different actors as it provides the basis for building stronger disaster response systems in the future and implementing measures that would prevent disasters from occurring in the first place, especially in the case of human-made disasters. The aim of this chapter is twofold: the first is to analyze the role of different local actors in disaster response and the interorganizational relationship that develops between them, especially where a weak state is involved and the second is to broaden the literature on the public sector corruption and mismanagement and its effect on disaster response.

This chapter will answer the following questions:

- To what extent did the corruption of the state affect the response on the ground?
- What is the long-term impact of local nonprofit intervention in post-disaster?
- Were organizations able to reach their response and recovery goals?

DOI: 10.4324/9781003222545-6

The main argument of this chapter is that the high level of bureaucracy and corruption have led to the failure of the government in both preventing disasters and managing post-disaster events, prompting associations and volunteers to assume the role of the state; it also argues that although different players stepped in to assist, they failed in their response due to the lack of cooperation and coordination as well as the lack of clear strategies for response.

To do so, the first section, "Beirut Explosion", provides a background of the events that led to the Beirut explosion; the second section, "Local Players in the Response Phase", will analyze the role of local players in responding to the disaster; the third section, "Challenges During This Response", will analyze the disaster management process in Lebanon and the chapter will conclude with the main findings and the impact on disaster response in developing context.

Beirut Explosion

Beirut's blast occurred during a huge transformation in the Lebanese state. Since October 17, 2019, Lebanon has experienced an uprising that called for transparency and accountability and the end of sectarian rule. It also came at a time when Lebanon faced a dire economic crisis. The unemployment rate was on the rise, and corruption in the public sector was at its peak. Prior to this uprising, different events had taken place: huge fires engulfed many territories of Lebanon and the government failed to respond to these crises, leading to the displacement of many families. Fuel and bread prices also increased and were lacking in the market. By August 2019, unemployment in Lebanon was at 25%. All these downturns happened because of mismanagement and the absence of proper state governance.

The final trigger for this uprising was a series of taxation policies mainly over WhatsApp calls. One month after the uprising, the economic situation in Lebanon started to collapse. The banking sector started falling apart, and in turn the poverty rate in Lebanon also increased, keeping in mind that all these factors preceded the COVID-19 pandemic. With the arrival of the first COVID-19 cases to Lebanon, the government decided to close the airport and create a state of emergency. In parallel, local communities, in cooperation with local governments, created "crisis cells" that were responsible for the management of the response to the pandemic and community assistance in different areas.

On August 4, at around 6 PM in the afternoon, Beirut was shaken by two explosions. While the first caused minimal damage, the second explosion, which took place less than five minutes later, was labeled by many as "Beirut-Shima" as its power obliterated the city. Approximately, 6,500 people were injured; 200 were dead; and 300,000 people became home-less, of which more than 80,000 children were displaced. The explosion destroyed the country's main grain silo, leaving Lebanon with less than three weeks' reserve of grain. Less than two hours after the explosion, vol-unteers from all parts of Lebanon poured into the area of destruction to provide relief to the different communities under distress.

According to the Human Rights Watch report investigation of the Beirut Port explosion, on August 4, 2020, the blast killed over 200 people, wounded and displaced thousands, caused significant damage to infrastructure and transport systems, incapacitated major healthcare centers, as well as triggered unquantifiable damages such as environmental or psychological harm (HRW, 2021). Citing the World Bank, the report noted that the explosion resulted in material losses that amounted to around $3.8-4.6 billion (HRW, 2021).

The explosion and the post-disaster response mirrored the incompetence and corruption of the ruling elite:

1. The explosion caused more than 12 billion dollars in damage in a coun-try with an already collapsing economy, further leading to an increase in the poverty rate.
2. The explosion was caused because of the storage of more than 2,700 tons of nitrate ammonium, without any regard for safety measures, since 2013. This material was on its way to Mozambique on a ship. However, because of legal complications, the cargo ended up docking and staying at the Beirut Port (Seibt, 2020). The 2,700 tons were trans-ferred to Warehouse 12 in the Port of Beirut. While the cargo should have been sold in an auction, this sale never happened.
3. Due to the highly bureaucratic system in Lebanon and the related opera-tional mismanagement, this material was left in Warehouse 12 for seven years. Port officials stated that they repeatedly alerted the Lebanese authorities to the dangers of keeping a stock of highly explosive prod-ucts in a single hangar close to the center of Beirut (Sbeit, 2020). The Lebanese court made six unsuccessful applications requesting permis-sion to dispose of the products. One of the letters in 2016 stated:

   In view of the serious danger of keeping these goods in the hangar in unsuitable climatic conditions, we reaffirm our request to please request the marine agency to re-export these goods immediately to preserve the safety of the Port and those working in it, or to look into agreeing to sell this amount. (Sengupta, 2020)

   Two days before the blast, many reports were sent to the president and the prime minister warning them that these products were dangerous and could cause a massive explosion in Beirut.

4. To add insult to the injury, there was no national statement issued to condemn the event and government bureaucrats were not sent to assist after the explosion. Forty-eight hours after the blast, the prime minister resigned stating: "corruption in Lebanon was 'bigger than the state' itself, and a very thick and thorny wall separates us from change; a wall fortified by a class that is resorting to all dirty methods to resist and preserve its gains" (BBC, 2020).

Indeed, this apocalyptic event highlighted the culture of negligence, corruption, and blame shift that characterizes the Lebanese bureaucracy, while highly depending on volunteers and the nonprofit sector to fill the gap. In this regard, the next section will analyze the role of different players in the response to disaster, mainly government agencies, the private sector, and the volunteers.

Local Players in the Response Phase

When analyzing the disaster response, the role of each player and their impact on the response should be discussed.

Government Role and Response

In terms of the direct response to the explosion, the affected area was directly secured to make way for investigative units and emergency response entities (El Sayyed, 2020). The state also assigned the assessment of the damage process to the Beirut municipality in collaboration with the High Relief Commission (El Sayyed, 2020). On August 13, nine days after the explosion, the government declared a state of emergency; the Lebanese Armed Forces were given the role of operational lead, noting that the government's capabilities were limited in terms of response resources (OCHA, 2021).

The Internal Security Forces along with the Lebanese Red Cross (LRC) were tasked with ensuring security, locating missing people, identifying dead bodies as well as unconscious injured individuals (El Sayyed, 2020). Additionally, the government officially joined the Lebanese Army and Ministry of Health in a committee to ensure the organization of medical requirements and handling of international donations and medical support (El Sayyed, 2020). To that end, the Beirut Forward Emergency Room (FER) was set up by the Lebanese Armed Forces in collaboration with the Lebanese Red Cross, as well as consultants, to oversee humanitarian support and development and rebuilding efforts (UN Office for the Coordination of Humanitarian Affairs) (OCHA, 2021, 10).

However, the HRW report (2021) underscores the government's minimal to nonexistent rescue and relief efforts on the ground in the immediate aftermath of the explosion as volunteers took on the tasks of removing rubble and rushing affected people to healthcare facilities. Indeed, the Lebanese government was not prepared for disasters and withdrew when the disaster took place. This lack of preparedness is due to the government's reliance on civil society to step in when disaster strikes; the government interference was meant to control rather than assist affected people. While it should have cooperated with organizations on the ground, the government did the opposite: through the policies it adopted, it jeopardized the response to the disaster. While literature argues that the government should cooperate with organizations, in Lebanon the contrary occurred: interorganizational relationships were absent in Lebanon, and this led to the lack of a proper response.

In the discussion of the Beirut Port explosion, it is impossible to overlook the reality that the disaster was avoidable and is, at least on the technical level, a result of criminal negligence and poor management (HRW, 2021). The Beirut Port is divided, in terms of management and benefit, among the ruling elite (HRW, 2021), which is where recommendations for avoiding disaster resulting from mismanagement should start. It is noted that several government officials were made aware of the explosive materials in the port and their potential hazards (HRW, 2021). Therefore, an initial preventative measure would be related to decreasing bureaucracy and ensuring that communication channels among officials are transparent and better documented. In addition, it is important to assign and divide responsibilities for concerned individuals and groups to take appropriate action upon receiving the information.

These preventative measures were visibly absent in the pre-existing government systems for handling crises and disasters. For instance, entities that were aware of the situation, such as military intelligence and the port management, did not take the necessary measures needed for the safe storage of ammonium nitrate, nor did they ensure that the repairs needed on the container were completed (HRW, 2021). As a result of the lack of hazard risk awareness and effective communications, members of the fire department were sent to the site of the fire and were not informed of the explosive material on site (El Sayyed, 2020). In that sense, restructuring the port, and to a larger extent the entire sectarian power-sharing structure of the Lebanese political system, becomes imperative for the prevention of disaster (Geha et al., 2020, p. 4).

Among the most important areas of disaster management is government effectiveness in coordinating with the healthcare sector for emergency response. The World Health Organization's strategic response plan report highlighted how the economic crisis in Lebanon exacerbated the aftermath of the port explosion, citing deficits in medication and equipment, shortages in hospital emergency response personnel, as well as the load of COVID-19 and associated safety measures (WHO, 2020). Although the hospital disaster plan was set in motion, hospitals that were still operational did not have the resources or actual space to admit the influx of patients in an organized and documented manner (Al-Hajj et al., 2021). In response to the unprecedented number of patients needing urgent care, hospital staff resorted to unofficial documentation and "interim triage", which refers to the prioritization of care for more urgent cases (Al-Hajj et al., 2021).

Role of Local Government

When discussing the response phase, it is important to assess the role of the local government: in this case, the role of the municipality of Beirut. The Beirut municipality had for its main function the coordination with the High Relief Commission to assess the damages (El Sayed, 2020). However, the municipality was absent from the affected area. Organizations were doing the work of the municipality and replaced the role of the local government, even the responsibility of removing debris and recycling them was ignored. Moreover, the policy adopted by the municipality hindered the work of associations, mainly the circular that stressed that initiatives and associations were not allowed to work without securing a pass. The municipality was not prepared for any disaster and even could not provide a map of the city of Beirut as the latest date back to 1976.

Role of the Lebanese Army

While the Internal Security Forces were the main designated agency to assist with searching for missing individuals, in addition to DNA identifications in coordination with the Lebanese Red Cross, and to securing the affected areas and protecting them from theft, the Lebanese Army was the main body responsible for coordinating the response phase.

Directly after the blast, the Lebanese Army closed the area and worked with the investigation teams in addition to the search and rescue groups. They created, along with the Lebanese Red Cross, and civilian consultants, the Beirut Forward Emergency Room. The main aim of this emergency room was to "manage humanitarian and development efforts in the afflicted areas, to rebuild them and support citizens", thus acting as the interface of the UN and humanitarian partners working in the area of the explosion (OCHA, 2021). Moreover, the Lebanese Army created an incident command structure responsible for the disaster response activities such as operations, logistics, planning, and finance. In addition to the above, the Lebanese Army and the Ministry of Health developed a liaison committee responsible for the prioritization of medical needs, overseeing donations in addition to coordinating the delivery of resources (El Sayed, 2020).

Moreover, a call center was created for all inquiries about the response activities and a task force was introduced to operate on disaster recovery activities, in addition to making sure that the unaffected part of the port remained operational to ensure the arrival of international aid. Simultaneously, the Beirut International Airport became the main designated area for receiving international aid (El Sayed, 2020). It is worth noting that all international aid directed toward Lebanon were channeled through either the Lebanese Army or the NGOs, since donors had lost trust in the government and preferred to directly assist these associations. While more than 400 organizations registered with the Lebanese Army, stating their interest in helping in post reconstructions, many others refused to do so (Fawaz, 2020).

NGOs and Private Sector

The human consequences of the explosions were such that the needs were beyond the capacity of the government. Thus, NGOs, private sectors, and volunteers stepped in to assist; they mainly focused on the relief process, mainly helping the displaced and affected individuals. Many donation funds were created on social media to support the initiatives (El Sayed, 2020).

In developing countries, governments neither have the financial expertise nor the know-how to respond to disasters, let alone building resilience. They rely on nongovernmental organizations to respond. Thus, local nongovernmental organizations often play a significant role in disaster response since a large category of NGOs is usually mainly concerned with disaster and relief work. Therefore, they tend to provide valuable support by virtue of their experience or knowledge in disaster response and by virtue of being familiar with the areas and populations they are trying to assist.

It was no surprise that following the Beirut explosion associations in Lebanon were the first to step in to assist. NGOs from all over Lebanon altered their missions and combined all their efforts to support the affected population. Since the first day, associations started cleaning the streets, providing food and shelter for the most affected areas; medical support was also provided. Associations started joining efforts working under one umbrella to ensure that people got the required assistance. Most of the organizations were local associations. From those organizations that stepped in, there were organizations that were already focusing on relief and reconstruction; however, other newer organizations shifted their focus to assist in the reconstruction efforts. After the Beirut Port explosion, NGOs mainly focused their efforts on people who were displaced or materially affected by the blast, partly by setting up crowdfunding and donation accounts to encourage several response efforts such as reconstruction, supporting shelters, providing care for children, and more (El Sayyed, 2020). However, according to the Action Aid report prepared by Bou Zeid and Abouchedid (2020), based on accounts by affected people and civil society organization members, civil society groups were not fully prepared to tackle the aftermath of the explosion, especially as most NGOs in Lebanon were oriented toward issues related to citizenship, development, education access, and gender. The effort of these NGOs was further exacerbated by the lack of initial documentation and needs assessments on the governments' part (13). For instance, a civil society representative from Rene Mouawad Foundation noted that food distribution was disorganized as it was done randomly at the beginning and then stopped because they wanted to base it on long-term needs assessments (Bou Zeid & Abouchedid, 2020, p. 13).

NGOs and civil society groups faced several additional challenges in their aid distribution efforts, caused by the government's absence in clear rural and urban mapping (Bou Zeid & Abouchedid, 2020). Therefore, these organizations resorted to municipalities and smaller-scale community representatives, many of whom were unreachable due to COVID-19 lockdown restrictions, to obtain the contact details and addresses of affected residents (Bou Zeid & Abouchedid, 2020). According to Bou Zeid and Abouchedid (2020), several false promise incidents were reported by affected people due to the presence of many civil society actors as well as spontaneous and independent volunteers. Both aid workers and affected groups pointed out the presence of what was referred to as "parasite organizations", who presented themselves as involved in the aid and rescue efforts, by, for instance, taking photos of themselves near repaired house areas that they did not contribute to take credit and secure funding (Bou Zeid & Abouchedid, 2020). Several affected individuals also expressed wariness around certain civil society actors and some women pointed out that certain NGOs came off as intrusive (Bou Zeid & Abouchedid, 2020, p. 14).

Aside from coordinating with municipalities and local community representatives, civil society members also worked with the Lebanese Army to facilitate access to "geographically divided zones", highlighting the strain imposed by the bureaucratic process involved in getting the Army's permission to impart relief efforts (Bou Zeid & Abouchedid, 2020, p. 20). Additionally, the government's minimal coordination efforts led to "duplications, overlaps, and redundancies such as providing the same type of aid to the same affected population repeatedly by different CSOs debilitating the efficiency of the humanitarian intervention" (Bou Zeid & Abouchedid, 2020,

p. 20). This redundancy was made worse by the fact that needs assessments were conducted by several different actors at the same time, described by an International Red Cross member as "assessment fatigue" (Bou Zeid & Abouchedid, 2020, p. 20). Coordination efforts were also strained by competitive behavior between NGOs to secure international funding, which can all be traced back to poor execution by the state in developing a coordinated national emergency response strategy (Bou Zeid & Abouchedid, 2020, p. 20).

Volunteer associations played a crucial role in the response. The Lebanese Red Cross, which was responsible for providing first aid and identifying victims, was deemed indispensable (Cheeseman, 2020). According to the International Federation of Red Cross and Red Crescent Societies emergency plan report, the Lebanese Red Cross deployed 75 ambulance teams and collaborated with 50 EMS center teams from areas outside Beirut for rescue efforts (IFRC, 2020, p. 2). Due to access restrictions making it difficult for ambulances to pass through, several makeshift treatment centers were created for emergency care, and four health centers and five medical mobile units were set up across Beirut to provide healthcare services, including treatment and medical supply distribution (IFRC, 2020, p. 2). The Lebanese Red Cross was responsible for evacuating two large hospitals that were affected by the explosion, as well as organizing blood drives, noting that they were able to secure 450 blood units by the next morning (IFRC, 2020, p. 2). The Lebanese Red Cross was also able to provide short-term housing for around 1,000 affected families, counselling services, as well as manage provision of hygiene supplies, food, and urgent cash support (IFRC, 2020, p. 3).

In addition, the Lebanese Red Cross played a significant role in conducting needs assessments. After preparing a three-month financial plan by August 5, the LRC later prepared a comprehensive year-long plan, mainly noting that the required budget would amount to US$125 million (IFRC, 2020, p. 3). Among the assessments prepared was the Multi-Sectoral Needs Assessment (MSNA), involving over 40,000 families, which assessed the vulnerability of affected groups, physical damage to houses, and conducted an overview of the socioeconomic status of affected families (IFRC, 2020, p. 4). Ultimately, the LRC's efforts in the aftermath of the blast cut across several sectors, from emergency aid, medical social support, blood transfusion, and disaster management, as well as providing support based on the needs of the affected population, ranging from shelter, food, as well as other necessities.

It is highlighted that there was an absence in financial support from the private sector to the Lebanese state due to the mounting lack of confidence in government institutions and considering the economic crisis as well as the explosion which is attributed to corruption and mismanagement on the government's part (El Sayyed, 2020). Among the initiatives that were launched as a result of the explosion was "Khaddit Beirut", which aimed to build a "roadmap for recovery that is evidence-based, community-led, and locally driven" (Geha et al., 2020, p. 11). The authors highlighted the difficulty associated with launching such an initiative due to the lack of similar disasters that could be used as a guide. However, this initiative succeeded in focusing their efforts on health, education, environment, and street reparations (Geha et al., 2020, p. 11).

NGOs also took on the role of dividing and assigning tasks, for instance directing volunteers and engineers to houses in need of repairs or reconstruction (Cheeseman, 2020). Additionally, several NGOs focused on communication and documentation, which was particularly challenging in the aftermath of the blast (El Sayyed, 2020). The government failed to adequately coordinate official status updates on response efforts, including information on "rescue operations, fatalities' identification, damage assessment, international assistance, and on other disaster recovery-related activities", which led NGOs to set up accessible databases and programs for missing people, unidentifiable individuals, and available resources such as food or housing (El Sayyed, 2020). Through their documentation, NGOs were able to secure the data needed for international support communities to identify priorities (Cheeseman, 2020). Tadamon al-Ness or "People's Solidarity", an organization formed in 2019 to support those suffering from the consequences of the economic crisis, had a database of around 4,000 independent volunteers who were ready to provide aid and relief efforts immediately after the explosion, for instance.

Associations adapted to working on the ground and shifted their missions to respond to the disasters. However, this led to a lack of professional response and duplication of work. While associations learned from their mistakes and tried to cooperate with each other, this cooperation was not successful with the absence of two major players, which were the local government and the central government. All associations stressed on the need for the presence of the government to succeed in the response to the disaster.

It is worth noting that most of the international aid was not directed at the Lebanese state and was instead distributed directly to civil society groups, hospitals, and UN entities due to the mistrust and lack of transparency associated with the Lebanese government (Renino, 2020). In fact, Transparency International's corruption perceptions index ranked the Lebanese state particularly low and gave it a score of 137 out of 198 countries (Renino, 2020). Among the other obstacles in the aftermath of the blast is the eruption of a fire in the port area on September 9, which halted Lebanese Red Cross and other rescue operations taking place, as well as the resignation of Hassan's Diab's government in the weeks following the explosion (Renino, 2020).

The private sector did not support any government agencies, mainly for the following reasons (El Sayed, 2020):

(1) Holding the government accountable for the unsafe storage of the nitrate ammonium.
(2) Loss of trust between the people and the government, mainly because of corruption and the financial crisis that hit the society.

However, while these organizations were the first to step in, the lack of coordination and planning led to the failure of the response to the disaster. This bottom-up approach to the management of the issue was faced with failure (Fawaz, 2020). A couple of months after the explosion, the area did not recover, and people were still homeless. While working on their own with a total absence of the state, associations in Lebanon were alone to respond to the disaster. The lack of cooperation and funding led to the failure to reconstruct the city.

Moreover, although these NGOs have the willingness, the funding, and the human resources to step in and replace the role of the state, they are also failing due to a lack of coordination, know-how, and support from the government. In this regard, a participatory approach to disaster should be adopted; the government should be the one providing full support and coordinating the work on the ground; associations should work more on collaboration and coordination of efforts on the ground. These will secure a proper response to disaster.

Volunteers

The work conducted by volunteers in response to the port explosion of August 4 and the following days is cited as the most significant contribution to relief work. A large portion of the volunteering effort, however, was not pre-planned or organized. Thousands of volunteers spontaneously flocked to Mar Mikhael and Gemmayze to aid heavily affected areas as they had little faith that the government would offer an effective response (Dadouch, 2020). Volunteers mainly focused on cleaning destroyed or partially destroyed houses and apartments by collecting rubble, wiping blood, fixing furniture, and even reorganizing belongings (Dadouch, 2020).

Cheesman (2020) noted that many volunteers handled donations for those who were affected. Volunteers also donated face masks, coffee, water, and food, while others guarded gates and entrances to prevent looting or theft (Dadouch, 2020). The volunteering effort extended beyond immediate relief, as some took note of the shortages that affected people suffered from and made sure to provide the right resources, such as missing medication or psychological support (Dadouch, 2020). Chehayeb and Sewell (2020) noted that volunteers created social media pages to match displaced people with host families and find them temporary shelter. Volunteers were also committed to ensuring the streets were cleaned and that the broken glass was recycled (Dadouch, 2020).

Therefore, a large portion of the humanitarian response effort was led by residents as individuals or as part of civil society, extending from local support to support from the Lebanese diaspora living abroad (OCHA, 2021). It is noted that the participation of several different entities led to some challenges in higher levels of coordinated response; however, these efforts proved crucial to the response strategy as they facilitated immediate support and flexibility (UN Office for the Coordination of Humanitarian Affairs (OCHA), 2021, p. 7).

Discrimination

The volunteering efforts were diverse, involving individuals and groups from different backgrounds, including the Palestinian civil defense volunteers who collaborated with Lebanese teams to rescue people from below the rubble (Chehayeb & Sewell, 2020). Migrant workers, Syrians, and Palestinians were also involved in the street clean-up effort taken on by volunteers, while other groups took on the role of providing food, shelter, and other necessities for migrant workers who were affected by the Blast (Chehayeb & Sewell, 2020). Although aid efforts were diverse, several reports indicated that aid distribution was noninclusive and, in many cases, prejudiced. Sukarieh (2020) shed light on the unequal distribution of aid based on class and citizenship, pointing out the oversaturation of volunteering efforts in middle- and upper-class areas, including Mar Mikhael, Achrafieh, and Geitawi where most of the affected were Lebanese. In contrast, other areas received less support from civil society organizations and the volunteering efforts were more scattered (Sukarieh, 2020). Although the aforementioned areas were not prioritized in the initial emergency response strategy, some civil society organizations noted that volunteers and NGOs faced access restrictions to certain communities under the control of political parties (Bou Zeid & Abouchedid, 2020, p. 17). In this case, NGOs reached out to civil society organizations that were politically affiliated to negotiate and take over (Bou Zeid & Abouchedid, 2020, p. 17). This type of exclusionary assistance sheds light on how preexisting sectarian divisions ultimately infiltrate emergency and aid work.

Affected groups expressed facing discrimination based on citizenship status, gender, and sexuality. Sukarieh (2020) noted that migrant workers from Ethiopia, Sri Lanka, and Bangladesh reported prejudice on the part of humanitarian aid workers. As highlighted in the article by Chehayeb and

Sewell (2020), the Lebanese Centre for Human Rights (CLDH) reported cases of selective aid distribution based on nationality or religious sect. Additionally, the Anti-Racism Movement (ARM) condemned aggression against Syrian residents by different groups and reported that the Internal Security Forces frequently requested that volunteers show their IDs (Chehayeb & Sewell, 2020). Some accounts by civil society organization representatives stated that certain donations were made under the condition that they be distributed to affected Lebanese residents specifically, which contradicts the inclusivity principle that underlines all humanitarian aid efforts (Bou Zeid & Abouchedid, 2020, p. 15). Many women also shed light on incidents of discrimination in terms of aid distribution, for example favoritism for those who have children, or rudeness and mistreatment by aid workers (Bou Zeid & Abouchedid, 2020, p. 17). On the other hand, civil society organization workers also reported discrimination and aggression, citing the incident in which members of the Relief Social Association were attacked by politically affiliated gangs in Zuqaq el-Blat (Bou Zeid & Abouchedid, 2020, p. 19). Aid workers also reported incidents of sexual harassment, and LGBT groups, such as Helem, faced discrimination as some civil society organizations initially refused to cooperate with them (Bou Zeid & Abouchedid, 2020, p. 18).

Challenges During This Response

More than 18 months after the explosion, despite international and local efforts to respond to the disaster, the area did not recover, and people are still homeless. Many have argued that the relief process was not successful: the lack of cooperation and funding led to the failure in reconstructing the city. Moreover, while NGOs were the first to step in, the lack of coordination and planning led to the failure of the response to the disaster. This bottom-up approach to the management of the issue was faced with failure (Fawaz, 2020), despite the quick response to the disaster coupled by engagement from the community. This disaster had a long-term consequence on the Lebanese society: all the immediate needs, mainly healthcare, food security, and protection, "exposed underlying structural ones, revolving around economic activity, livelihood opportunities, and social security". Indeed, many challenges were present during this response phase: while many international donors responded by sending field hospitals, their functions, locations, and roles were not coordinated with functioning hospitals and thus it was visible that the need was more in supplies and medication as opposed to medical personnel or hospitals (El Sayed, 2020). Another major challenge was related to public information and communication. Indeed, there was a highlight about the lack of clear official status reports covering response activities, including rescue activities, fatalities numbers, damage assessment, and international assistance (El Sayed, 2020). This gap was filled by different NGOs that "launching public databases for missing individuals, unidentified victims, lists of available resources (food and shelter), and so forth". It is important to highlight that this disaster happened during COVID-19 pandemic. The pandemic added to the challenges that the healthcare was undergoing since two of the major affected hospitals were also treating COVID-19 cases. The government responded with a clear incident command structure, and gaps were filled by the private sector and the community.

Reviewing the role of the state, Lebanon failed with disaster risk reduction (DRR) policies. This failure could have been avoided had the Lebanese state followed the guidelines of DRR: although Lebanon designed risk reduction strategies, it failed to issue proper policies to implement them. Indeed, although signatory of the Sendai Framework for Disaster Risk Reduction (2015–2030) in addition to the 1994 Yokohama Strategy and Plan of Action for a Safer World and the Hyogo Framework for Action 2005–2015, Lebanon failed to prevent the Beirut explosion, due to the lack of implementation of the provisions of these frameworks.

For example, clause 27g of the Sendai Framework asks all member states to "establish and strengthen government coordination forums composed of relevant stakeholders ... and a designated national focal point for implementing the [framework]" (Mahfouz & SynSapien, 2021). Moreover, the 1996 Yokohama strategy also called for the establishment of "clearly identified bodies charged with the promotion and coordination of disaster reduction actions". However, since 1990, the Port in Lebanon has been managed by a temporary committee that does not report to any minister. Thus, there is an absence of an executive power that exercises power over the area. The parliament has yet to pass the draft law on the establishment of a DRR in Lebanon. However, due to consociational system in Lebanon, this law is still in the drawers of the parliament. In return, in 2009, the then prime minister established an ad-hoc unit that is directly linked to his bureau (Mahfouz & SynSapien, 2021).

When deciding on the usage of the nitrate of ammonium at the port, there was an absence of a clear authority to decide on what to do with the material. Thus, none of the different players in the government had the capacity and/or the willingness to decide on how to deal with these explosives. In such situations where the decision-making process is divided between different players, Sendai Framework clearly states the need for "a strong foundation in national institutional frameworks with clearly assigned responsibilities". Moreover, according to the Sendai Framework, there is a need to "promote the resilience of new and existing critical infrastructure, including water, transportation and telecommunications infrastructure".

Had this framework been implemented, the authority in Lebanon would have directly pinpointed that it was not prepared to handle such dangerous goods, and the Beirut Port did not have a location to handle dangerous cargo.

In addition to the above, clause 30-c of the Sendai Framework called for "promoting mechanisms for disaster risk transfer and insurance, risksharing and retention and financial protection". However, in 2011, the Lebanese government argued in a report that one of the main challenges for an efficient DRR was "inherent absence of allocated funds in the national budget for recovery and reconstruction" (p. 19). Additionally, the report stated the importance of developing a "partnerships for reconstruction between the public and private sectors, through insurance programs" (p. 20). Yet, to date, nothing has been executed and most of the insurances are refusing to pay until the end of the investigation (El Sayed, 2020).

Thus, Lebanon has failed in its role in the different phases of disaster management.

(1) At the mitigation level, the Lebanese governments and agencies did not identify the risks associated in the storage of the explosive chemicals, especially that this fertilizer had already caused a huge accidental explosion in the past. All these agencies failed to create awareness to reduce these risks. As a result, this led to the Beirut Fire Department of Beirut to respond without any knowledge of what was stored (El Sayed, 2020). Moreover, at the time of the incident, there was a failure in notifying the public and protecting the communities living in the affected zone: hospitals, citizens, and operating businesses were not notified of the potential threat (El Sayed, 2020), keeping in mind that "a disaster management authority in charge of risk assessment, hazard identification, and disaster response is missing in Lebanon because the disaster response draft law that was submitted in 2012 to the Lebanese Parliament has not been approved to date" (Mursheid, 2015).

(2) Moving to the second phase of disaster management, the response rate, the incident command center was created, and the Lebanese Army took over the command of the response phase. However, the major issue faced by the government was the appeal of the private sector and the communities to bypass the government agencies mainly due to the political and financial crisis that the government was undergoing (El Sayed, 2020). Thus, the international coalition pledged US$200 million directed toward the population and requested reforms from the government (BBC News, 2020).

Studying the political administrative and economic system in Lebanon provides a clear picture behind the failure of the Lebanese government in preventing and responding to disasters. Since its independence, Lebanon has lacked all the main components to become a state with functioning bureaucracy. The corruption and nepotism affected the state in delivering the basic utilities such as water, electricity, and garbage collection. Moreover, ministries and municipalities do not fulfill their mandate: on the contrary, governmental institutions became an arena for nepotism at the expense of passing and implementing broader developmental projects. The dysfunctional bureaucracy led to corruption and nepotism and prevented the state from developing clear disaster management strategies. The socioeconomic policies adopted by the state did not provide the proper ground for the society to develop hazardous events are bound to happen in the absence of clear infrastructure. Moreover, the strong civil society organizations that are replacing the role of the state are transforming it into passive players in disaster management: the reliance on associations has led the Lebanese state to withdraw from post-disaster phase without providing proper effort or assistance needed for coordination.

Linking these factors to the literature discussed in Chapter 3, it is clear that the (1) failure of the government, the (2) low GDP and bad economic policy coupled with the (3) lack of cooperation and main strategy from the part of civil society organizations led to absence of clear disaster mitigation and response in Lebanon: the state failed to develop a clear strategy for disaster preparedness and response. Moreover, local NGOs and initiatives faced several challenges that affected their performance during the response to the Beirut Port explosion.

Inequality in Funds

To compensate for the gap of the government and its inability to invest, Lebanon always counted on the help of the international community. The international community helped Lebanon without going through the traditional process and instead of transferring donations via the government, international donors preferred to help people through local NGOs (Macaron, August 2020). Even though this process helped affected people receive help, this created a huge gap between local and international NGOs and between local NGOs receiving international help and other local NGOs not receiving the same help (Mirshad, August 2020). Furthermore, local NGOs receiving international funds did not cover all the affected sectors. For instance, few were the initiatives that focused on ensuring the basic needs of women with all the economic situations affecting the country in parallel with the explosion (Mirshad, August 2020).

The Increase in NGO Numbers

The response to the Beirut Port explosion witnessed a proliferation of NGOs and initiatives. On the one hand, this growth accelerated the response to the explosion and increased the number of beneficiaries. However, two main problems resulted from this proliferation. First, a huge number of assessments were done by different NGOs with the same affected population (Self, 2021). This duplication of work created a sense of resistance from the beneficiaries who expressed their irritation with these continuous visits. Second, the proliferation of NGOs directly after the explosion and specifically their rapid response, left behind a lot of undone work or weak work. This absence of quality work was due to the focus of NGOs to increase the number of beneficents in their reports. Both consequences turned out to be challenges for local NGOs to proceed with their work as without the trust of beneficiaries and without professionalism local, NGOs cannot act.

On the other hand, the proliferation of local NGOs and initiatives created question marks in terms of the transparency and accountability of these NGOs. The timeline in which these NGOs were created was so quick that their accountability was questionable in terms of how they registered in this small timeline (Ghantous, 2021). In fact, many of these NGOs were not registered and many of these were not professional as they did not report where the money given to them was spent. International funders became reluctant to send funds and intensified their standards and requirement.

The Absence of Central Command and Unpreparedness

One reason for the failure of the response to the Beirut Port explosion by local NGOs was the lack of coordination between them and the absence of a central command to ensure a successful response (Ghantous, June 2021). In fact, the absence of the state created a chaos in the organization of the work conducted in the affected area. Consequently, the state was represented by the Forward Emergency Room (FER) unit led by the Lebanese Army. However, NGOs were disoriented on whether they should refer and report to the FER unit or to the international organization platform, mainly the one led by UN agencies (UNDP, UNHCR) (UNHCR, September 2020).

This chaos disturbed and slowed down the work of local NGOs, especially the newly established ones that did not have an adequate number of members. Local NGOs had to report to both the FER unit and the UNDP unit. Moreover, due to the lack of communication between NGOs, a lot of duplication was done. This duplication was a waste of resources, and a part of the affected population was left without any help. Duplication was due to the weak assessment done by NGOs and to the noncommunication of data between NGOs. However, due to the weakness of the program used and the lack of technical capabilities that hindered the application of the program, the Lebanese Red Cross could not manage the deduplication process. The Lebanese Red Cross was one of the biggest NGOs that received international funds and distributed them adequately (LRC, 2020). The LRC developed internal coordination groups and external coordination groups and took the lead in the multiple sector national assessment (OCHA, April 2021). In addition, the LRC helped the UN and its partners to receive updates on the humanitarian gaps that resulted from the explosion, but the LRC needed a further assistance from the UN (LRC, 2020).

Thus, after the explosion, local NGOs were not the leaders. Instead, international NGOs were the leaders of the response to the explosion because they were the ones deciding the repartition of resources and favoring one NGO over the other. Local NGOs were also excluded from the decision-making meetings held by international organizations to coordinate the funds and donations to Lebanon (Self, May 2021).

Many platforms were created to coordinate the work between NGOs and to organize the distribution of resources on the ground; however, the diversity and the number of these platforms hindered the success of local NGOs in coordinating the response to the explosion.

The Lebanese Economic Crisis

Local NGOs were always the first to intervene after any kind of disasters in Lebanon. However, the deterioration of the Lebanese economy mainly translated into the devaluation of the Lebanese lira, challenged local NGOs, and restrained their resources. These financial constraints forced local NGOs to wait for the international aid. Furthermore, the banking sector crisis imposed a limitation on the amount of money that Lebanese citizens could withdraw. This restraint further complicated the process of welcoming donations or accepting and withdrawing donations that came through the bank. Without money, providing the needed resources was impossible without international aid. This long and complicated process challenged the success of local NGOs in the response to the explosion because it slowed it down and made it highly reliant on international communities and Lebanese diaspora.

The Pandemic and Healthcare Sector

After the explosion, Lebanese citizens forgot about the pandemic and took to the field to help each other through the crisis. However, the occurrent pandemic rendered a part of the society hesitant to help, especially as the healthcare system was already drained. After the explosion, the healthcare sector was one of the most affected sectors, accessing medication and hospitalization was difficult. Therefore, accessing healthcare services, providing shelters as rehabilitation, and ensuring the livelihood of the affected population were the three sectors in huge need of emergency (ACAPS, August 2020). However, priorities went for repairing damaged doors and windows to ensure that people have houses and homes where they can find refuge.

Conclusion

This chapter analyzed the Beirut explosion and the mismanagement of the crisis through the lenses of disaster management and corruption in the light of the presence of a strong civil society. It argues that four different factors affect the response of the state: failure of the bureaucracy, lack of a presence of clear disaster management strategy at the national level, an economic crisis that led to increasing poverty rates, and the lack of cooperation from civil society. This chapter demonstrated how the Beirut explosion highlighted the failure of the Lebanese government in its disaster management and mainly mitigation and response phases. And how local NGOs and initiatives faced several challenges that affected their performance during the response to the Beirut Port explosion.

Linking these factors to the literature discussed in Chapter 2, it is clear that the weakness of the Lebanese state and administration led to the absence of clear disaster response in Lebanon: the state failed to develop a clear strategy for disaster preparedness and response. Moreover, it illustrated how the lack of coordination and cooperation on the part of the different players on the ground, coupled with competition over the international fund, negatively affected the response rate. Although organizations tried to bypass the role of the state and directly intervene on the ground, this proved to be a wrong strategy. To be able to have a clear mitigation strategy, a holistic and participatory approach should be adopted: levels of corruption should be reduced, economic strategy should be adopted, and civil society should be included in the national disaster strategy. Only then would the Lebanese state be able to have a holistic approach to disaster management and response.

References

ACAPS. (2020). *Emergency operations center Beirut assessment & analysis cell analysis of affected areas in Greater Beirut*. ACAPS. Last modified August 12, 2020. https://www.acaps.org/sites/acaps/files/products/files/20200812_acaps _secondary_data_review_beirut_e.

Al-Hajj, S., Dhaini, H. R., Mondello, S., Kaafarani, H., Kobeissy, F., & DePalma, R. G. (2021). Beirut ammonium nitrate blast: Analysis, review, and recommendations. *Frontiers in Public Health, 9*, 657996–657996. https://doi.org /10.3389/fpubh.2021.657996.

BBC. (2020). Beirut explosion: Lebanon's government resigns as public anger mounts. https://www.bbc.com/news/world-middle-east-53722909.

Bou Zeid, M., & Abouchedid, K. (2020). Participation of local and international civil society in the Beirut blast response. ActionAid: Arab Region. https:// reliefweb.int/sites/reliefweb.int/files/resources/beirut_blast_policy_brief_single _pages_final.pdf.

Cheeseman, A. (2020). After Beirut explosion, Lebanese volunteers flock to help clean up. *NBC News*. https://www.nbcnews.com/news/world/after-beirut -explosion-lebanese-volunteers-flock-help-clean-n1236403.

Chehayeb, K., & Sewell, A. (2020). Local groups step up to lead Beirut blast response. *The New Humanitarian*. https://www.thenewhumanitarian.org/news -feature/2020/08/18/Lebanon-Beirut-explosion-local-aid-response.

Dadouch, S. (2020). They return to homes damaged in Beirut's blast to discover someone has already cleaned them. *The Washington Post*. https://www .washingtonpost.com/world/middle_east/they-return-to-homes-damaged-in -beiruts-blast-to-discover-someone-has-already-cleaned-them/2020/08/10 /85c3bda0-db04-11ea-b4f1-25b762cdbbf4_story.html.

El Sayed, M. (2020). Beirut ammonium nitrate explosion: A man-made disaster in times of the COVID-19 pandemic. *Disaster Medicine and Public Health Preparedness, 1–5*. https://doi.org/10.1017/dmp.2020.451.

Fawaz, M., & Harb, M. (2020). Is Lebanon becoming another "republic of the NGOs"? Beirut *Urban Lab*. https://www.beiruturbanlab.com/en/Details/697/is -lebanon-becoming-another-republic-for-ngos.

Geha, C., Kanaan, F., & Saliba, N. A. (2020). Breaking the cycle: Existential politics and the Beirut explosion. *Middle East Law and Governance, 12*(3), 357–368. https://doi.org/10.1163/18763375-12030007.

Ghantous, G. (2020). Beirut port blast death toll rises to 190. *Reuters*. https://www .reuters.com/article/us-lebanon-crisis-blast-casualties/beirut-port-blast-death -toll-rises-to-190-idUSKBN25Q08H.

Human Rights Watch. (2021). They killed us from the inside. An investigation into the August 4 Beirut blast. *Human Rights Watch*. https://www.hrw.org/report /2021/08/03/they-killed-us-inside/investigation-august-4-beirut-blast.

International Federation of Red Cross and Red Crescent Societies. (2020). *Emergency plan of action operation update Lebanon /MENA: Beirut port explosions*. IFRC. https://reliefweb.int/report/lebanon/lebanonmena-beirut-port -explosion-operation-update-report-n-4-mdrlb00.9

Lebanese Red Cross. (2020). *External evaluation - Cash response port Beirut explosion*. Lebanese Red Cross. Last modified 2020. https://www.redcross.org .lb/wp-content/uploads/2021/09/LRC-BPE-CVA-response-External-Evaluation -report-Sep-2021.pdf.

Macaron, J. (2020). Lebanon is on track to become a failed state. *Al Jazeera*. Last modified August 7, 2020. https://www.aljazeera.com/opinions/2020/8/7/lebanon-is-on-track-to-become-a-failed-state.

Mahfouz, B., & SynSapien (2021). How implementing Sendai could have saved Beirut. *PreventionWeb*. https://www.preventionweb.net/blog/how-implementing-sendai-could-have-saved-beirut.

Mirshad, H. (2020). Grassroots groups hold Beirut together, yet big NGOs suck up the cash | Hayat Mirshad. *The Guardian*. Last modified August 27, 2020. https://www.theguardian.com/global-development/2020/aug/27/grassroots-groups-hold-beirut-together-yet-big-ngos-suck-up-the-cash-lebanon.

Murshed, Z. (2015). *Strengthening disaster risk management capacities in Lebanon*. Outcome Evaluation Report. Beirut: UNDP.

OCHA. (2021). *The humanitarian response to the Beirut port explosions Lebanon flash appeal 2020 – End report*. ReliefWeb. Last modified April 30, 2021. https://reliefweb.int/sites/reliefweb.int/files/resources/end_of_fa_report.pdf.

Renino, R. (2020). Beirut blast disaster response: International aid and grassroots mobilization. *Twai*. Last modified October 9, 2020. https://www.twai.it/journal/tnote-88/.

Seibt, S. (2020). The strange history of the chemical cargo that caused the Beirut blast. *France 24*. https://www.france24.com/en/20200807-the-strange-history-of-the-cargo-that-caused-the-beirut-blast.

Self, J. (2021). Impacts of Covid-19 on the relationships between local and international humanitarian actors: The case of Lebanon and the 4 August 2020 Beirut port explosions. *Diva Portal*. Last modified May 2021. https://www.diva-portal.org/smash/get/diva2:1564030/FULLTEXT01.pdf.

Sengupta, K. (2020). Beirut explosions: Lebanese authorities failed to deal with explosive stockpile – despite knowing risks. *The Independent*. https://www.independent.co.uk/news/world/middle-east/beirut-explosion-news-lebanon-authorities-stockpile-kim-sengupta-a9655766.html

Sukarieh, R. (2020). Disaster aid distribution after Beirut explosion reflects Lebanese societal divides. *The Conversation*. https://theconversation.com/disaster-aid-distribution-after-beirut-explosion-reflects-lebanese-societal-divides-144627.

UNHCR. (2020). *UNHCR flash update on Lebanon: Beirut port explosions*. UNHCR - The UN Refugee Agency. Last modified September 20, 2020. https://www.unhcr.org/lb/wp-content/uploads/sites/16/2020/09/200920-UNHCR-Flash-Update-on-Lebanon-final.pdf.

World Health Organization. (2020). *Beirut port blast emergency strategic response plan*. http://www.emro.who.int/images/stories/lebanon/who-lebanon-strategic-response-plan-27.9.20.pdf?ua=1.

Conclusion

Disasters are sudden events that directly interrupt the daily lives of the affected population and produce human, economic, and environmental losses. Since these disasters usually overwhelm the resources of the affected state, many international, regional, and local actors step in to assist in the relief process. During the response phase, these international actors are restricted by humanitarian principles; moreover, irrespective of the political, social, and economic status of the donor state, the intervention should be based on humanity, impartiality, neutrality, and independence. However, the response from international donors is never the same: when intervening, these latter usually allocate assistance based on their agendas and policies. Thus, international aid is not only based on humanitarian response; other factors are also taken into consideration: strategic, political, and economic concerns. Moreover, affected countries differ in their socioeconomic status and global influence, and as such the global relief responses also differ in their donations, initiatives, and responses to these disasters. This means that the decision to donate and the amount of the donation would be determined based on the extent to which this humanitarian aid would advance the donors' agendas in the affected country. In this case, donations would not be need-based, falling out of line with their guiding principles. In this regard, this book argued that the response to disasters should be viewed from an international relations lens; indeed, foreign policies influence the allocation of funds, and the decision to assist is based on strategic considerations.

As Chapter 2 argued, international actors differ in their responses. While regional organizations provide financial and technical resources, international nongovernmental organizations focus more on providing relief and play the role of linking donors to recipients. They are considered as major actors that lead the response and can adapt to the environment where they are functioning. They usually have budgets that might exceed the budget of corporations and states. However, in many instances, they might represent the interests and agendas of the donors and the states, and this in return negatively affects the humanitarian response and the allocation of funds.

Diasporas are becoming major players at the international level through their mobilizing resources and raising awareness about the affected areas. The efficiency and effectiveness of the assistance are usually questioned since most diasporas are not experts in disaster response or do not have an objective view of the needs of the affected community, and most of the resources are usually directed to one activity, which signifies a lack of proper planning for disaster recovery. It is also argued that the remittances they send, on some occasions, affect political accountability as they allow certain groups to rule despite their failure in proper governance in their areas of power.

However, the major actors in disaster response at the international level remain donor states, especially since most of the international assistance comes from western states with the United States being in the lead followed by Japan and France.

In responding to disasters, states usually focus on increasing their powers. Thus, this study analyzed those responses from an IR theoretic perspective and realpolitik school of thought, which argues that when responding to disasters, the foreign policy agendas are based on the first securing the state resources and trade markets; hence, when disaster strikes, ex-colonial powers usually focus on assisting their ex-colonies. Moreover, this assistance is also based on political considerations such as foreign policies and domestic policies of the donor state in addition to internal politics of the recipient state; moreover, the internal governance of the state and the level of transparency and accountability also affect the decisions of the donor states: indeed, when institutions are weak, assistance is directed toward NGOs and multilateral organizations. Geographical locations, trade policies, and peer pressure also affect the decisions of the donor states to respond and assist when disasters strike. In poor and developing countries, international actors play a crucial role in disaster management, especially where disaster expertise is lacking. In the absence of financial and nonfinancial resources, assistance from countries and international players becomes crucial for disaster survivors in building resilience. However, this supply-driven reliance on international donors could lead to weak governance within local institutions, limited commitment from the state, and disordered decision-making at the local level.

When it comes to local players in disaster response, as Chapter 2 argued, the interplay of power among different actors and the uneven balance of power leads to new governance approaches. While there is a long-standing literature on state nonprofit relationships, few studies address the relationship that develops during disasters between these two actors. When reviewing this relationship, one should analyze the concept of "trust" between the different stakeholders. This trust is based on the performance of the public institutions: if these institutions already suffer from a bad reputation, this level of trust will be reduced when disaster strikes. This study has demonstrated that to secure a successful disaster response plan, different involved actors, being state and nonstate actors, should work on building trust between each other. In addition, they should have a clear coordination process based on a participatory approach. To do so, public institutions should introduce an administrative mechanism that permits the inclusion of different nonstate actors in the coordination process. However, the response phase is usually hindered by the level of corruption from the level of the state. Indeed, corrupt states are the most affected when disaster strikes since they have a low level of management to disasters, mitigation, and infrastructure, nepotism, and clientelism.

Moreover, those disasters would accentuate the corruption of the state due to the misuse of aid, international funds, and remittances sent by the diaspora. While local governments should be the major coordinating body in the disaster response, in developing context this later usually fails in this role as they usually allocate low priority and budget to develop comprehensive disaster mitigation plans; moreover, the rigidity of the bureaucratic systems makes the reallocation of budget to respond almost impossible. Thus, in such cases, it is volunteers and local associations that are stepping in to fill the lack. However, the lack of knowledge and preparedness, in addition to the lack of coordination with state actors, makes these responses a failure in many instances.

To illustrate the above, this book analyzes local and international responses to the explosion that happened on August 4 in Beirut, Lebanon, and reviewed the role of the different actors in this response in the light of a weak Lebanese government.

While Lebanon is prone to many disasters, as Chapter 3 argued, the political system of the state and the inefficient disaster management policies led the state to fail in its disaster response in many instances. Indeed, public administration in Lennon is facing many challenges, especially that it is intertwined with sectarian politics. The consociational democracy in Lebanon allowed the development of the culture of nepotism corruption and patronage in the public sector. The Lebanese administration is facing many governance problems that make it unresponsive to citizens' needs. While many international initiatives were directed to help the Lebanese government on the issues of transparency, these were faced with deadlocks. All anti-corruption laws that were introduced in Lebanon were always faced with many limitations. This in return is mirrored in the socioeconomic status of the state that has led to a lack of providing the basic needs for the citizens and an increased poverty rate in the state.

All these administrative weaknesses have also affected the capacity of the central and local governments to build clear disaster mitigation plans. While Lebanon has a disaster management program that dates to 1970, this authority does not enjoy any decision-making authority. Indeed, many constraints prevented Lebanon from developing clear disaster risk reduction plans, these being political, institutional, and related to human resources and gender discrimination. Most of these disaster management strategies did not include nonstate actors, especially nongovernmental organizations; in every disaster in Lebanon it was these associations that were stepping in to assist. These latter usually requested the help of international actors such as humanitarian organizations, NGOs, state, diaspora, and private sectors.

When the August 4 Beirut explosion occurred, different players stepped in to fill the gap left by the weak Lebanese state, being international and local. This case study is the best example that illustrates how responding to disaster is based on functional cooperation strategies used to advance the interest of different players. Indeed, as Chapter 4's findings demonstrated, the international assistance was mainly based on strategic and political reasons and highlighted the weakness of the Lebanese government. It illustrated how the assistance and sometimes lack of assistance by the international community mirrored the weakness of the Lebanese states as well as power struggle at the international level.

While many international players intervened in the response, each player intervened differently: the international humanitarian community did not have any political agenda; however, it lacked a clear strategy to respond. Their main concern was to transfer the aid directly to affected areas and NGOs on the ground as opposed to the government; in their view, the government could not properly respond. However, this strategy negatively affected the work on the ground, as NGOs started competing over the funds and negatively influenced the coordination on the ground.

The EU interference was also crucial and viewed that further deterioration in Lebanon would lead to regional instability. The weakness of the state led the World Bank and the EU to introduce a 3R model: reform, recovery, and reconstruction framework – with the main aim being to ensure that funds are distributed properly. However, this model restricted the assistance to the Lebanese state until it introduced institutional reforms. As Chapter 4 illustrated, this plan altered relief efforts as funds were stopped and negatively affected the response phase.

Another player was the Lebanese diaspora present all over the world. They played a crucial role in this intervention and created awareness about the need to assist Lebanon; however, it was short-termed and did not have a long-term impact.

Donor states were the major actors in this response. While neighboring states did assist, this assistance was very limited as compared to the intervention in previous disasters in Lebanon. This was due to three major issues: (1) the internal politics of the Lebanese state, (2) these states had different political agendas where Lebanon was not on the priority list, and (3) the lack of trust in the Lebanese administration that was tainted with corruption.

On the other hand, western states were the ones that played a major role; indeed, the major state actor was France. This state was among the first actors to intervene, and Chapter 4 stressed on the humanitarian and political roles. The research highlighted the importance of the French interference from a humanitarian point of view. This intervention, as the findings of Chapter 4 illustrate, was based on political and humanitarian considerations: the French wanting to reconfirm that Lebanon is important to them, especially due to the historical relationship between the two states, and to assert their role as major players in the region.

However, this intervention was also faced with failure in the long term since first the intervention plan was not well-grounded, and the second because the reform project presented by the French president was faced with resistance from the Lebanese ruling class to the project.

Hence, this research demonstrated that international intervention is indeed not purely humanitarian but is contingent on a strategic decision. Moreover, the internal politics and the weak institutions were major decisive reasons whether to provide direct assistance or not. This research highlighted how the Lebanese political scene directly affected the role of international actors.

Considering the above, Chapter 5 analyzed the role of local actors and the mismanagement of the crisis through the lenses of disaster management and corruption. In a corrupt state like Lebanon, the response to a disaster might not be as simple as it seems. The involvement of the government is minimalist and the willingness to collaborate and create interorganizational and cross-sectoral relationships is not clear. It argued that four different factors affected the response of the state: failure of the bureaucracy, lack of presence of a clear disaster management strategy at the national level, the economic crisis that led to increasing poverty rates, and the lack of cooperation from the side of civil society. Moreover, this study highlighted the need for coordination and cooperation between different actors on the ground. It further argues that government should have a clear economic strategy and clear plan that includes the NGOs. Only then will disasters be able. Chapter 5 concluded that to be able to have a clear mitigation strategy, a holistic and participatory approach should be adopted: level of corruption should be reduced, the economic strategy should be adopted, and civil society should be included in the national disaster strategy; only then the Lebanese state will be able to have a holistic approach to disaster management and response.

In conclusion, this research highlighted that disaster responses are indeed not independent from international relations and diplomacy; and any international decision to assist or not is based on geopolitical and strategic causes. The international community plays a crucial role in disaster response; each actor follows a different strategy. However, in developing contexts, this intervention becomes more crucial. The economic and social impacts are crucial. However, since these interventions are based on political and strategic issues, they are faced with failures in the long term. Strong interorganizational relationships are crucial in responding to any disaster. The Beirut explosion was the perfect example of the importance of such a strong relationship between the different players. Responding to disasters involves the responsibilities of international actors, the government, and local nonstate actors. In a weak state such as in Lebanon, the government alone cannot handle a response due to a lack of capacities or lack of intentions. International and local nonstate actors alone cannot intervene to fill the gap and provide the needed services to the affected community bypassing the state; there is the need to build trust between the different players. Effective responses are thus directly related to interorganizational and cross-sectoral relationships during a disaster. Building trust, communication, and collaboration between different local and international players are a necessity to successfully respond to any disaster.

Index

For Product Safety Concerns and Information please contact our EU
representative GPSR@taylorandfrancis.com
Taylor & Francis Verlag GmbH, Kaufingerstraße 24, 80331 München, Germany